# Make Your HarmonicaWork Better

## How to Buy, Maintain and Improve the Harmonica from Beginner to Expert

by *Douglas Tate*

Foreword by *Larry Adler*

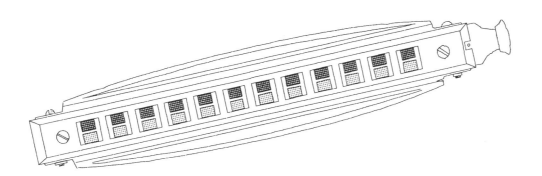

Cover Art - Used by permission of Hohner Inc.
and special thanks to Toni Radler

Cover Scanning - Shawn Brown
Production - Ron Middlebrook

ISBN 978-1-57424-062-7

Published by CENTERSTREAM Publishing
P.O. Box 17878 - Anaheim Hills, CA 92807

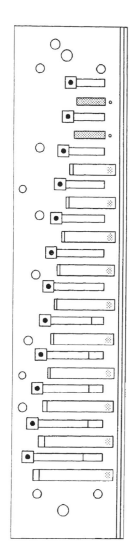

There is nothing difficult at this stage and the work only demand care and a little patience. The vast majority of player/fiddlers could stop at this point and be thoroughly satisfied with the results.

Level Three is for the player who does not mind experimenting and possibly making a mess of a couple of bits and pieces before getting it right. You will need more care and will possibly learn a thing or two about the use of hand tools in the process. Don't be put off. It's fun! Most people have a couple of harmonicas sitting in a drawer which they have given up all hope of ever being able to play. These are the ones to experiment with before working on your super De Luxe Stradivariety.

### Secrets

Many amateur players think, and say, that the great players have 'secrets' which enable them to get a rich sound, that they have 'special instrument'. Not so! Most of the great players started with and still use the standard instrument. What they *have* got is many years of experience derived from hard playing, listening to themselves and others, and being obsessively critical of themselves and their playing. (Very few players who are fond of their sound ever make it to the top!)

In the last couple of decades (1970 on) the situation has changed. Custom instruments with bodies made of various metals, professionally produced harmonicas with bodies of Plexiglas, silver, stainless steel, aluminium alloys etc. have changed the picture. The very best of these give a wonderfully stable platform for the reed plates and a superb chance for the maker to display art and skill in the production of a better instrument. Some say that the sound is not as good as that of wooden bodied instruments.

Tommy Reilly and Larry Adler play metal instruments,
Toots Theilemans and Harry Pitch play wood.
Who can argue with either?

## Maintenance before you've played it?

### The New Instrument

There are many tutor books which start off with how to look after your harmonica. The majority of the advice given is good if sometimes a little impractical. Lets look at a few things you can do to prevent things going wrong straight away.

Most instruments work when they leave the factory. Contrary to popular belief and to what I said earlier, the manufacturers would really like you to be able to play their instruments. By the time the harmonica arrives in your hands, however, it will have travelled a considerable distance, been transferred through a number of extremes of temperature and humidity, and, if handled by the Post Office, bashed about gently. (The little notice you put on your parcel saying 'Please handle with care' is not really of any use when buried in a sack being thrown on top of a pile of other sacks!) The result of the travels is that there is a possibility that things have been knocked out of place or just plain dropped off. This is not all that common. Most instruments are in pretty good condition when you get them.

When the shopkeeper gives you a new instrument, inspect it. Is the box or case OK? Does it show any sign of handling damage? Is the instrument still wrapped in its original paper, uncrinkled? Has it been on display? If it has do not accept it if it shows evidence of having been in a sunny shop window. (bleached looking box, curled flaps and even possibly a cracked body) If there are any signs that the instrument has been played, don't accept it. I would hate to think of you getting my dread Thuringian lung and foot rot. Look inside the mouthpiece for this evidence. Finger marks on the cover plates only show that someone else has handled it. If the shop has a set of bellows ask if you can test each note to find if they all work. (If the assistant tells you to try blowing the instrument, flee!) Don't attempt to fill the shop with sound from the bellows, just enough pressure to make sure the reeds work. Make certain that the slide works easily with no 'hard' points in its travel Check that the button end of the slider is not bent. Check that the coverplates show no obvious signs of bending out of shape. Check the cover supports. Are they bent?

If the instrument is new and in good condition and the shopkeeper is still smiling, don't try to beat the price down too much. We need people like that to stay in business.

## Now that you have your brand new instrument, how should you treat it?

"RUN IT IN LIKE A NEW CAR."

Most harmonicas have a beautiful free feeling when they are brand new and there is a temptation to let rip. DON'T. The flaps (valves) have not settled on the surface and there are air leaks. Because of these leaks there is a tendency for you to blow harder and this can cause the reeds to be over-stressed. The running in period is not long hours of playing, but numbers of times of playing with a reasonable gap in between. This method allows 'deposits ' to build up on the flaps and gives them a chance to shape themselves to the reed plates. With wooden harmonicas it allows for the gradual absorption and drying out of the wood. After a while the body does not absorb quite so much as the pores in the wood become filled with 'gunge'! If you start off with one gigantic session whilst swilling down many litres of beer, then the poor thing does not stand a chance. The body will swell and the lower two or three holes will cease to play as the reeds hit the side of the slots.

If you are a 'dry' player then your problems may be with playing. The 'wet' player will have troubles with the instrument .. and with playing!

At the start of a session try to make certain that the harmonica is at about your own temperature. Carry it in a little bag in an inner pocket, or like a piccolo player, under the armpit! A cold instrument allows moisture to form on the reed

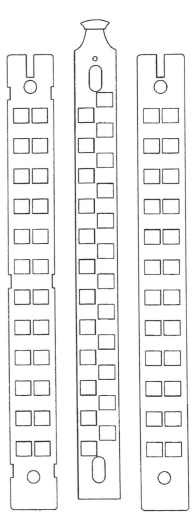

5

# Make Your *Harmonica Work Better*

*BE PREPARED TO*

*MAKE MISTAKES*

*AND RUIN A FEW OLD*

*INSTRUMENTS ..*

*The rest of us have,
so why shouldn't you?*

plate which makes the flaps stick. This will nearly always happen with flaps on the outside of the reed plates, which is lucky. Do not get it up to temperature by putting it on a radiator, the flaps will curl .. permanently.

"WARM GENTLY (!) IN YOUR HANDS"

Good advice which is almost universally ignored. Plastic bodied instruments tend to suffer from internal condensation. It is not usually very serious but you can get beads of condensation shifting onto the blow reeds and causing a burble.

"MOST MOUTH ORGANS SEEM TO TAKE 10 - 20 MINUTES TO BECOME USED TO THEIR PLAYER BEFORE THEY GIVE THEIR BEST"

True? I think that it is the player warming up a lot and the harmonica warming up a little. Runners warm up before a race, singers warble a bit, so maybe we need to do something similar.

"AT THE END OF A SESSION TAP OUT THE INSTRUMENT IN THE PALM OF YOUR HAND"

Not a bad idea, but if you can tap moisture out of the instrument after a longish play there is something seriously wrong with the way you are playing or you have a real 'wet' problem. I don't know a cure for this, but here is some advice. Do not use wooden bodied harmonicas. I've seen some really disgusting fungal growth inside wet players instruments. Plastic or metal is better here.

"WIPE THE INSTRUMENT BEFORE PUTTING IT AWAY"

See above. This is up to you. If you are the sort of person who has a nice tidy desk then you will no doubt wipe your instrument afterwards because you are methodical. My desk is chaos.

"AVOID HIGH AND LOW TEMPERATURES"

Final bit of advice in this section. The harmonica likes the same temperate conditions that we do. Avoid dropping or knocking it on a hard surface. This can upset the reed settings, bend the covers, move the slide movement and mouthpiece.

*ALWAYS USE COMMON SENSE.*

## A Harmonica Health Warning

All of the techniques described below work for me and many other people. However...

DO BE PREPARED TO MAKE MISTAKES AND RUIN A FEW OLD INSTRUMENTS ..

The rest of us have so why shouldn't you?

DO THINK EACH PROCESS THROUGH BEFORE STARTING ANY WORK. DO KNOW WHEN TO STOP.

Best do an alteration and find out how it works rather than alter all your instruments and find that you are a complete schmuck with tools. Mainly, take care, have fun, enjoy and eventually love that beautiful instrument.

## General

There are processes which you will be asked to perform in several of the sections which may need explaining. These are described here so that you can go through the book in any order and still understand what is being asked of you without repeated explanations.

### Tools

Below you will find a long list of tools which will be useful when you come to maintain or improve your harmonica. In an ideal world you would have the lot. You can get away with less!! However, the best tools are only just good enough. I have some favourites. Tommy Reilly gave me an extremely good set of small screwdrivers and a very powerful magnifying glass many years ago and they have been invaluable. Good stuff lasts and works! Go to a hardware store which caters for craftsmen if possible. Avoid places where everything is shrink wrapped.

To start with you will need a set of small screwdrivers, often sold as watchmakers or jewellers. These have a little revolving pad at the blunt end which helps you to hold and rotate them comfortably.

Good quality 150mm and 300mm metal rules. Get the type which has the markings cut into the surface. Use white paint on the surface and then wipe it off, leaving the cut marks full of paint. This will help reading the markings. Alternatively an anodised aluminium rule usually has a white surface with dark markings. They are not so accurate, don't last as long, are prone to damage, but are far easier to read.

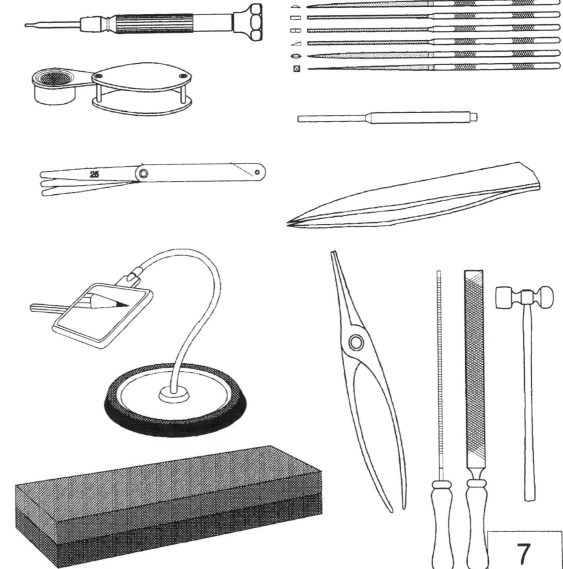

7

# Make Your *Harmonica* Work *Better*

A flat surface. Kitchen tables, spouses and harmonicas do not mix, be warned!. Get yourself a piece of stable chipboard about 200 by 300 mm and 20mm thick (or more). Bigger is better. It needs to have something like a laminated surface but avoid the worktop material which has a surface texture, you want perfect flatness. Cover the underneath with felt to stop it slipping. Even better is to glue four flat softish pencil erasers to the underside.

A few sheets of 240, 400 and 800+ grit Wet & Dry Carborundum paper. There are a variety of these papers, most are OK. ..experiment. You will be able to get them in car accessories shops at a pinch. Do not get the cloth types, they are useless for this job.

A set of needle files. These come in sets with up to about 10 to 12 different shapes and coarseness. Here are some shapes you will find useful: square, flat, triangular, round wedge. Be warned, a good set is quite expensive.

Some fine-cut, medium sized, parallel bodied files. Try and get some with one side flat for most of its length. The width should be so that it is nearly the same width as the slider. This is where your real hardware store will be able to help. If you have no good local store use the 'Yellow Pages' (Business telephone directory) to find a tool distributor or manufacturer and pester their sales people, you may even get a free sample!

A first class, double sided fine/coarse Carborundum stone about 200mm long and 70 wide. You will need a can of light machine oil as well to lubricate it. This oil is sold as sowing machine oil or Three in One. Anything heavier is not really good for this job.

A pair of medium to small flat bladed pliers. Try and get a pair which do not have serrations on the inside of the blades

A light weight hammer might come in handy. Get a ball peen (100 - 200 gram) type, you don't want it too heavy.

A pin punch, small enough to punch out rivets. Just under 1mm diameter.

A block of beeswax. You can buy it pure from the chemist, but I use the cheaper stuff from a woodworkers shop. I don't think bees produce two grades.

A drill of some kind. I use a small hand drill for most jobs. That way you can feel the drill cutting and have a little control. Some people have a good drill press, a stand with a drill head and motor, but this costs a few bucks! The compromise of using a motorised hand drill on a hobbyists drill stand is not good if you wish to retain the sensitivity of your ears!

A set of drills in millimetre sizes. Don't go cheap here. Cheap drills drill funny shaped holes. And, yes, you can actually drill a triangular hole with a badly sharpened drill bit.

A tube of glue. The type made for model aircraft is good. You can get non-stringing versions of this. There is nothing worse than fitting a valve and having hairs of glue clogging the next reed. It's not expensive, my last tube lasted over twenty years!

A pair of sharp pointed or flat ended tweezers. You can get these at a stamp shop or chemist, or any female dressing table.

A good stand magnifier. Get one with a rectangular rather than a round lens. Make certain that it has a firm base. You will get one at a good optician at a high price. Try to shop around. Optician supply houses will sometimes give you a better deal if you can get to them.

Essential .. A good high magnification hand lens. These are usually a very thick lens in a metal shell which folds into its own metal casing. This is valuable when you want to see exactly what the set of a reed is. Again an optician will supply. I found a very high quality but cheap one at the Royal Society for the Protection of Birds. So it may be a good idea to keep your eyes open for bargains.

A set of feeler gauges. The ordinary ones sold for car maintenance are good enough. The set will range from about 0.0015" to 0.025" (0.005mm to 0.1mm)

Some form of clamp to hold your board steady on the table (with newspaper under it please!).

You might like to glue a 'cage' of small pieces of wood to the board to hold the Carborundum stone steady when you are sweating over a hot mouthpiece.

This sounds like an awful lot of expensive gear. I have accumulated mine over the years and you most likely have a fair collection of bits as well. You don't need all of it but it helps to have most.

## Using the oil stone

Whenever an oilstone is used it should be lubricated with thin oil. (see above) If you do not lubricate, the stone gets clogged up with the cut metal and ceases to cut. At the start of any session lightly cover the surface of the stone you are going to use with oil. Rub it in with your fingers and then wipe off lightly with a cloth. This will remove any loose metal particles. Put another small puddle of oil on the cutting surface from time to time as you use it. It is fairly obvious when this is needed.

Different metals need different lubricants, but you can feel fairly safe for all the materials you are likely to use on the mouth organ with the oil mentioned above. Do try to avoid wearing grooves in the oil stone. Try to cut over the complete surface, turning the stone frequently (end to end and both sides).

## Using wet and dry paper

If you are using wet and dry paper on wood make certain that the paper is dry and has not been used wet. I would always keep a whole sheet of about 240 grit paper for use with wood, it seems to be about right. If you use any finer paper you will find that it clogs too quickly. After a few strokes with this paper brush off the wood dust to prevent clogging. An old nail brush is ideal for this job. If you use the paper this way it should last a very long time (years?). Possibly the best way to use wet and dry paper is to lay it flat on a surface and rub the object over it. This way the paper will stay flat and cuts flat.

Always use it wet when working in metal (there is one exception mentioned later in the text). This will make it cut better. When you begin a session, soak the paper in lukewarm to cold water for a few minutes before using it. If you do this the paper will last longer. The idea of the water on the paper is to float the debris from between the grit particles. Keep it and the object you are dealing with wet. At the end of a session, leave the paper flat to dry. It will try to curl up, let it. At your next session the initial soaking will straighten it out again.

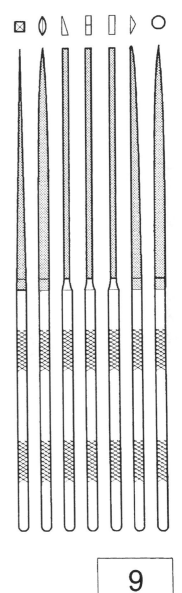

9

# Make Your Harmonica Work Better

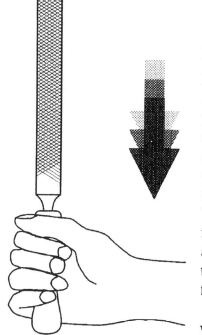

### Using a file

There are two main types of file you will be using. Needle files which have a built-in metal handle. 'Normal' files, which are normally sold without a handle, you have to buy and fit one.

NOTE... If you use a normal type file, you MUST use it with a handle. If you don't you run the very real risk of getting the sharp tine stuck in the base of your hand. (Read the industrial statistics on this sometime, its frightening!) How to fit a handle is not at all obvious. Ask for an appropriately sized handle at your hardware store. When you look at it you will find that there is a small hole in the right place for the tine. Push the tine home as far as you can comfortably. Now to do the non-obvious. Hold the handle with the file pointing vertically upwards. Bring the handle end sharply down onto a good solid table or the floor. You should now not be able to get the handle off the file!. What happens is that the handle stops suddenly and the file carries on driving into the handle. If you try to tap the file into the handle with a hammer it will just fall off after a while.

Always use a file lightly, never try to force it to cut. If you do force it you will cut inaccurately.

### Breaking corners

Whenever you drill a hole or file an edge there is a very sharp corner left on the material. Most times this is just what you want. However, in this book you will be asked to 'break' some of these sharp edges. All this means is that the extreme sharpness is taken off by a couple of strokes of the file or sweeps of the wet and dry paper. Don't overdo this as there are times, especially with the slide movement where too much can ruin the whole thing. Little is good!.

### Holding in a vice

Vice jaws are hard and certainly harder than any part of the mouth organ. You must be careful if you hold anything in the jaws that it is not clamped too tightly. If you do it may distort. The second point is that most vices have serrated jaws, little points, in order to help grip things. This will leave small pimple marks all over the place if you are not careful. It is not a bad idea to make a couple of pieces of bent cardboard (cereal packet is fine) to put over the jaws. This will protect and give a much softer grip. Only ever grip as tightly as you need to prevent movement.

### Lubrication

Things like springs etc. need a little lubrication. This is to ease the normal wear and tear between metal objects and also to give some rust protection to the steel parts. The amount of lubrication is usually stated in this book, but in general a small amount is best. The ONLY lubricant for the harmonica that I have mentioned (not for the oilstone) is Vaseline. This is a petroleum jelly. As it is a jelly made for plastering all over the human frame, I cannot think that the small amounts you will be using will bring you out in spots and give you fits. Only ever use it as a smear, not as gobbets. Always wipe off any surplus. In the past I have tried various silicone lubricants etc. but Vaseline is the one to use.

## Using Beeswax

This substance is used for filling in small cervices in the harmonica. All right! If the workmanship is perfect there would be no crevices. You are not perfect, the manufacturer is not perfect and I most certainly am not perfect, this stuff helps to give the impression that we are better than we are!

The best way to use it is with a small soldering iron. Use the iron to melt the beeswax and dribble it on to the part to be sealed. Be quite generous as it shrinks on cooling.

Let the stuff set hard before trying to remove excess. A thumb nail or a wooden spatula makes a good wax remover when you have made a fillet of the stuff. Scrape with a blade to make a flat surface. You will be left with a smear of the wax in places you don't want it. Use an old, dry flannel or a towel (that texture) and polish it off. The surface will be very slightly waxy but this is no bad thing. It disappears very quickly. (Beeswax has been used as a substitute for chewing gum)

## Bits and Pieces

No, not odd items, but what to do with the bits when you take the harmonica to pieces.

It is a good idea to make a series of little boxes to hold the various screws, buffers, covers, flaps etc. which you will take off. The boxes only need to be a few millimetres high to prevent things wandering. Too deep is bad in any case as you will not be able to get a things in the small boxes otherwise. Get a piece of cardboard (cereal packet again) to glue all the boxes onto.

Label the boxes so that you always have the same bits in the same place. Make a couple of slotted racks so that you can stand both the reed plates on end. This way the setting of the reeds doesn't get altered and the flaps don't get bent. It is not a bad idea to make compartments for things like your small screwdrivers, scribe, glue, magnifying glass, rule, screws etc. This will make certain that you know where they are when you want them!

It is a good idea to have pad of paper handy to write down notes about what you are going to do, what you have done and when. You can also jot down things that you notice about the settings of the reeds and the stickiness of the flaps whilst you are playing. That way you don't have to be continually putting the thing back together again to remind yourself of the sound while doing the alterations. Put a small bit of Blu-Tac on the end of your pencil, it is great for picking up screws, flaps etc..

## Lighting

You will need a well lit area to do any work on the harmonica. You simply cannot get away with poor lighting when doing fine work. You really need a good multi-source light. A single source tends to give troublesome shadows. I usually work with a couple of 'angle-poise' type lamps so that I can adjust them when necessary. The 'new' low power bulbs give a very good soft, but bright, light for repair work. (You may need to beef up the springs on your Anglepoise lamp if you use the low energy bulbs, they are heavy).

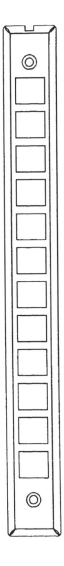

11

## Cleanliness and sharpness

Do keep your hands as clean as possible during the work. Wash them at intervals. You will collect all sorts of glue, grease and bits on your hands. If these get onto the reeds or flaps you will have trouble.

Keep your tools clean. Don't let them lie in piles of rubbish. Treat tools with respect and wipe them down when you have finished using them.

Keep your tools sharp. A friend of mine is lazy. He sharpens the tool he is using every few minutes. That way it cuts easily, that way he cuts accurately, that way he doesn't sweat. Lazy man .. brilliant craftsman.

Work on a piece of paper or lint free cloth whenever possible. Change it or shake it out frequently to get rid of muck. A clean work area really helps you to work well.

## Tools .. Again

I have dealt with this earlier but this advice cannot be overemphasised.

Do not skimp on your tools. Get the best you can afford. Have fewer of top quality rather than a lot of rather mediocre ones. When you buy quality tools they will last longer and cut better. Do not mistake price for quality, consult an old fashioned hardware store or hand-tool seller. Ask for advice from somebody who really knows what they are talking about. Take time. I am still using tools I had as an apprentice 40 years ago. They cost me what seemed like a lot of money then, but it has been repaid time and time again.

# Mouthpiece

## Function

To guide air from the mouth to the appropriate reed slot.

To make the contact between the player and the instrument efficient and comfortable

## Shape

This varies. Some have square holes, some round, one has square with rounded corners.

There are two main profile shapes. A truncated triangle which butts onto the slide movement. An extended truncated triangle with a skirt which butts onto the cover plate and an integral slot which contains the slider pieces.

## Materials

Usually a moulding in a nickel plated brass. Silver plating is used in some more expensive models. Gold plating has been used for show rather than function but it wears quickly.

## Maintenance

During manufacture the mouthpiece is intentionally bent to ensure pressure along the length of the slide movement. If this has been done enthusiastically it can lead to air leaks (see section on alterations to the mouthpiece later in the book).

Sometimes the underside hole edges obscure a portion of the slide holes resulting in reduced airflow.

On some models the underside edges and corners are very sharp and can cut. These can be rounded

Slightly undo the retaining screws, ensure that the mouthpiece is central on the slide movement. Tighten the screws until they are 'finger tight'. This gives correct pressure.

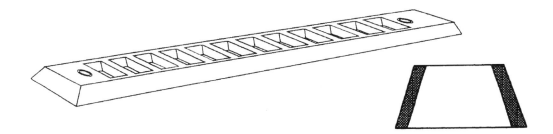

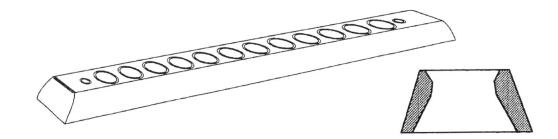

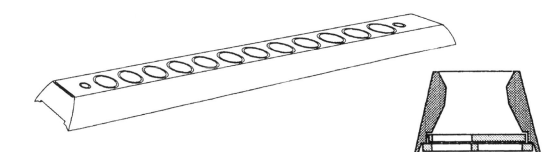

13

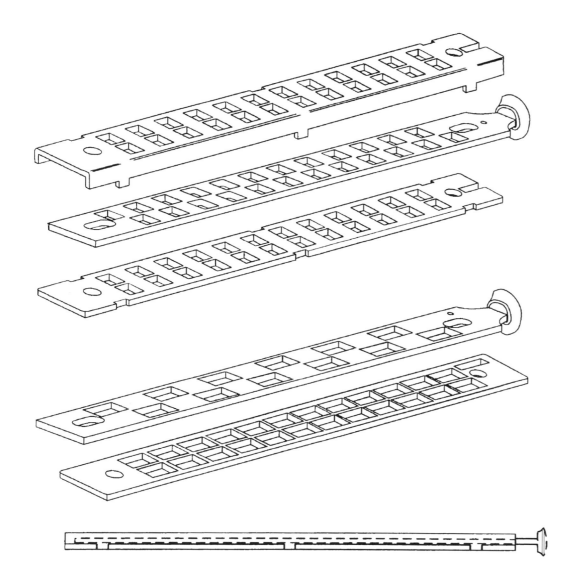

# Slide Movement

## Function

To guide air, from the player, through the mouthpiece to the appropriate layer of the instrument, upper or lower, and thus to enable playing in any key.

To help provide a seal between body slots, the reed plates and the cover plates.

## Shape

There are two main types, long and short movement, and two construction methods, 3 piece and 2 piece.

The long movement is used to allow larger holes and thus more air flow than the short movement type. The shorter movement allows easier control of the slide.

## Materials

Usually a  nickel plated, brass based material. More expensive instruments sometimes use stainless steel which may be coated with PTFE plastic (nonstick).

## Maintenance

Check that the slide movement as a whole is centralised on the body by slackening the mouthpiece screws, adjusting and re-tightening.( see Mouthpiece )

The slide becomes stiff sometimes due to deposits of dried saliva. With wooden bodied models you must remove the slide mechanism, wash in soapy water and then reassemble. Metal and plastic bodied instruments may have the front dipped in clear water and the slide pressed a few times to dissolve deposits. Tap out and wipe dry afterwards.

# The Slide Button

## Function

To provide a cushion for the finger at the end of the slider.

To allow holding of the slider when precise control is needed.

## Shape

There are many different shapes. Unfortunately most seem to have been designed for cosmetic appeal rather than function.

## Materials

Various types. Nickel plated turned brass is the most common. The Hohner Silver Concerto has a solid silver knob and there is one example of this with a ruby inset into it. The Amadeus has a slider button which is gold plated.

## Maintenance

No maintenance required.

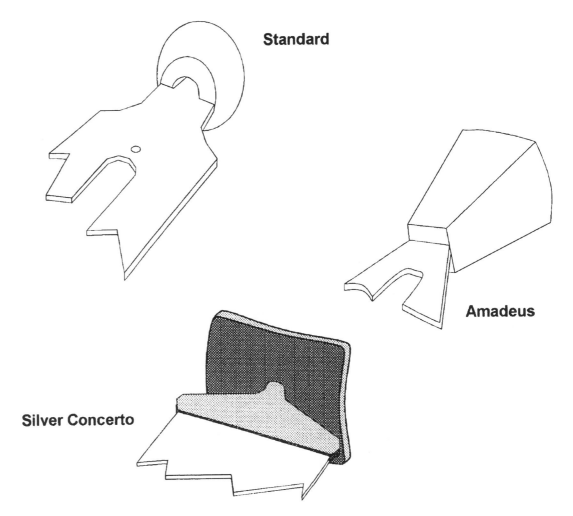

Standard

Amadeus

Silver Concerto

15

# Slide Buffers

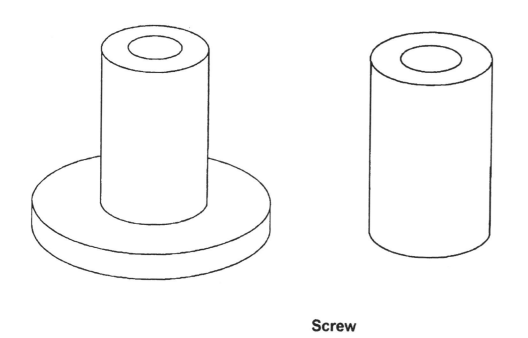

### Function

To provide a soft and cushioned end stop for the slider mechanism.

To help keep the position of the mouthpiece and slide movement stable relative to the body.

To stop the slider hitting the mouthpiece holding down screws.

### Shape

There are two basic shapes. The majority of instruments use a simple tube shape. The Amadeus harmonica has a T shaped tube.

### Materials

The standard material is a type of Neoprene, a soft clear plastic with great resilience and resistance to surface cutting from the slider.

The Amadeus buffer appears to be made of a type of rubber and is prone to be destroyed by the slide in a very short time.

An emergency material can be the plastic ink tube from a cheap ballpoint pen.

### Maintenance

No regular maintenance.

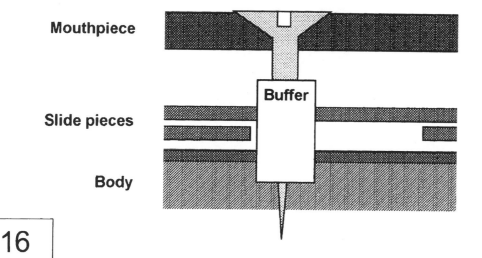

**Screw**

**Mouthpiece**

**Buffer**

**Slide pieces**

**Body**

# The Spring

## Function

To provide a means of returning the slider to its home position as quickly as possible after use.

To provide positive positional feel when using the slider to 'half slide' notes.

## Shape

Usually two straight or slightly bent arms joined by either 2 or 3 coils of the material.

## Materials

Spring steel wire approx 0.075mm diameter (0.030") A domestic safety pin can also be used.

## Maintenance

This spring is prone to rusting and should be coated with petroleum jelly (Vaseline) every week. The weekly treatment can be a smear on the top of the spring where it appears through the slider. The whole spring should be taken out and treated about once a year.

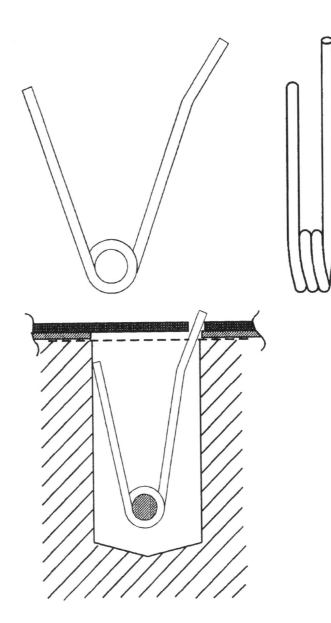

17

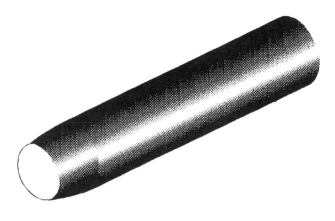

# The Spring Post

## Function

To provide a stable positioning platform for the slider spring to work from.

## Shape

In most of the mass produced instruments this is a simple rod positioned by holes in the reed plates and body.

In some metal bodied instruments a metal screw is used with a plain section for the spring to rest on.

Another method used is to mould the post into the body material. This is done more on the plastic and aluminium bodied harmonicas.

## Materials

Mild steel rod or a turned screw of plated brass or steel.

## Maintenance

Occasional lubrication occurs when spring maintenance is done.

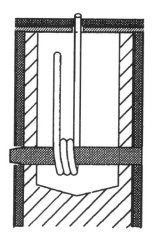
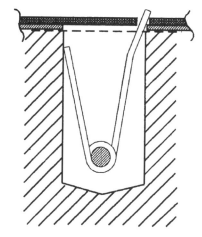

# The Body

## Function

To provide a stable platform for all the other parts of the instrument.

To provide air guides from the mouthpiece / slide assembly to the pairs of reeds.

## Shape

The body consists of a series of shaped slots in a solid material. The actual shape depends on the material used and whether it is machined, cast or moulded. The Amadeus has the body material extended beyond the back of the cover plates for artistic effect.

## Materials

Traditionally this is wood. Many types of wood have been tried but all suffer to some extent from the moist atmosphere inside the instrument.

Recently bodies have been made from moulded plastic, Plexiglass and a variety of metals. Metals used have mainly been solid silver (instrument grade). anodised aluminium

## Maintenance

No easy maintenance possible.

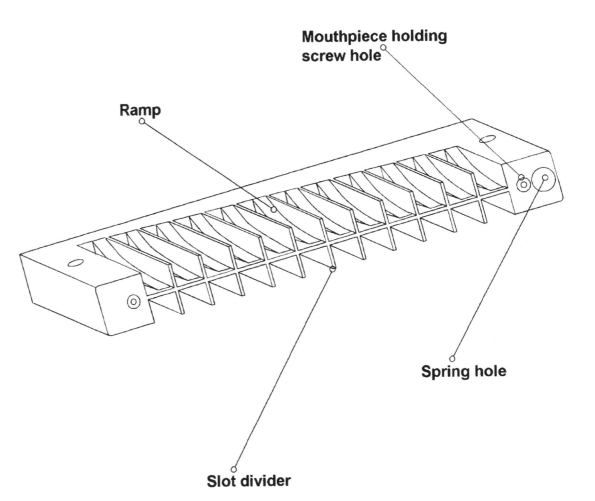

Mouthpiece holding screw hole

Ramp

Spring hole

Slot divider

# Reed Plates

## Function

To provide a stable platform for reed fixing and wind saving valves.

To provide accurate, close fitting slots for the reeds to vibrate in.

To affect tone and volume of the reeds by the thickness of the plate.

To provide a seal between slots and body.

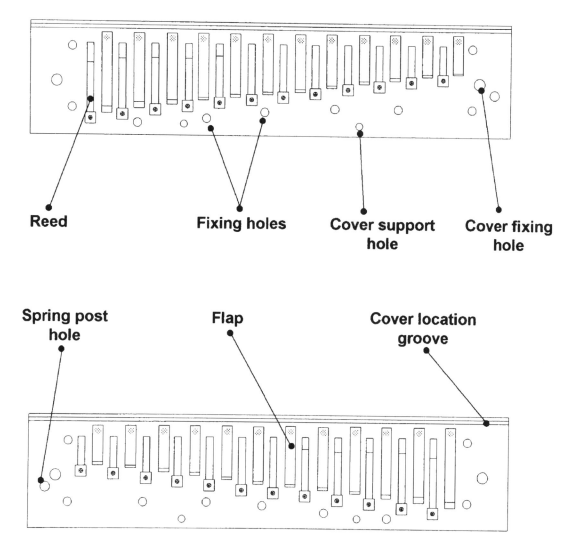

**Reed**     **Fixing holes**     **Cover support hole**     **Cover fixing hole**

**Spring post hole**     **Flap**     **Cover location groove**

## Shape

Most harmonicas have the oblong, slotted plates the same size as the body and sitting on top and underneath it. Some have the plates slightly smaller and sitting in recesses in order to aid positional accuracy.

## Materials

Usually brass based. Thicker plates than standard have been made of coated aluminium or aluminium alloy for extra volume but these corrode easily. There are possible health hazards from Aluminium. The main reason for using this material is that it is soft and therefore easy to punch slots in.

## Maintenance

No regular maintenance needed.

# Reeds

## Function

To provide sound by vibrating when air forces the reed to bend into its slot.

To provide a fixed pitch sound which is dependant on the material, its stiffness due to hardening, length, width, thickness, how the thickness varies along its length and the size and shape of the 'blob' weight on the free end. (note that this fixed pitch can be varied downwards by up to a tone or more by skilled players.)

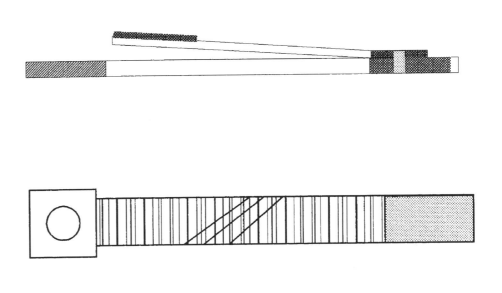

## Shape

On commercial harmonicas the reed is universally a parallel cantilever with thickness which varies in a variety of ways along its length. The fixed end always broadens into some sort of pad with a fixing hole for the rivet in its centre. This hole is usually punched out of the material and tends to leave a dimple.

The outside shape is achieved by stamping out of a sheet. The profile by a grinding operation. This is later changed again slightly by a tuning operation

## Materials

Copper based materials are used (like phosphor bronze). There are two main types, the standard and a much softer version used to make 'long life' reeds.

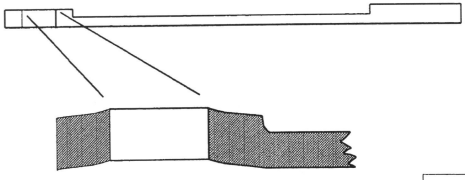

## Maintenance

Occasional tuning.

21

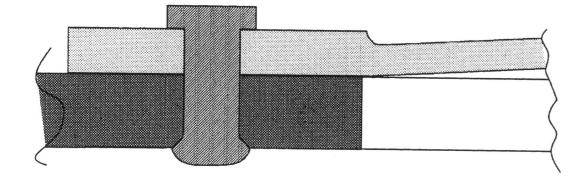

# Rivets

## Function

To hold the reed accurately and firmly in a precise position.

To clamp the reed holding pad so that the there is no vibratory movement of the pad itself

## Shape

The rivet shape depends on the manufacturer. It is usually a piece of rod with a small head on one end. The reed is put in position, rivet threaded through the reed and plate, the free end of the rivet is then 'hammered into shape to form another small head.

Sometimes small screws are used instead of rivets. This can be of great advantage to the player if carefully assembled.

## Materials

These are frequently made of mild steel and rust as a consequence. More expensive instruments sometimes use a more rust resistant material.

## Maintenance

None.

# Wind Saving Valves (Flaps)

## Function

To prevent air escape through the reed plate slot not being played in a particular pair of reeds. The action of stopping the air has to be as fast and noise free as possible.

To lift from the reed plate with no sticking to the surface when its associated reed is sounded.

To be insensitive to sympathetic vibration with the pitch of the note being sounded or any of its harmonics.

## Shape

A single piece of paper-like material. Glued to the back of the rivet and just overlapping the reed slot. Mostly this has a second independent stiffening layer added.

## Materials

The primary flap is made of a soft floppy plasticised paper-like material. The secondary flap is usually a plastic, much more rigid and springlike.

The underside of the primary flap usually has a slightly roughened undersurface to help prevent sticking.

Sometimes the flap is made of leather and has no secondary spring.

## Maintenance

Preventative maintenance only. Do not overheat the instrument otherwise the flaps will curl.

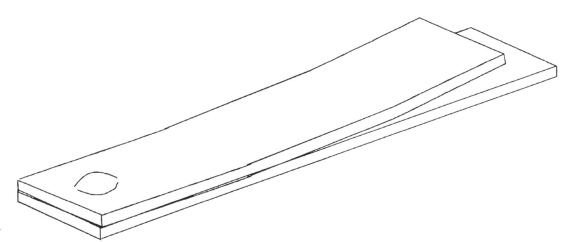

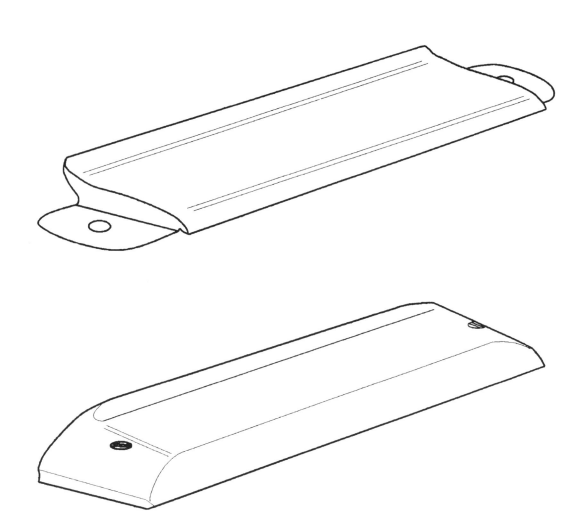

# Cover Plates

## Function

To provide a primary soundbox.

To provide an acoustic coupling between reeds and the outside air (or hands).

To provide a stable platform for holding the instrument.

To provide a continuation of the mouthpiece for the players mouth.

## Shape

Frequently considered a cosmetic accessory rather than an acoustic necessity. The shape is rarely ergonomically correct although some come close. The ridge at the back of most covers provides stiffness and also a holding point.

## Materials

Traditionally nickel plated brass. Sometimes these are silver plated to good effect. Gold plating has been used less effectively because of wear. Recently stainless steel has been used to good effect as the base material.

## Maintenance

No regular maintenance. Wiping after playing is a good idea if you are a damp player.

# Cover Posts

## Function

To provide support for the cover plates to avoid crushing by the players fingers during playing.

To help provide stability for the primary soundbox.

On more advanced instruments to provide tensioning adjustment to enable tuning of the cover plates.

## Shape

On many instruments these are merely a flattened stamping of brass with a sharp point to allow hammering into a wooden body.

Some instruments have more substantial turned, rod shaped posts which either screw into the reed plate or metal body through a hole in the reed plate.

## Materials

Nickel plated brass sheet, turned nickel plated mild steel or turned stainless steel.

## Maintenance

No regular maintenance.

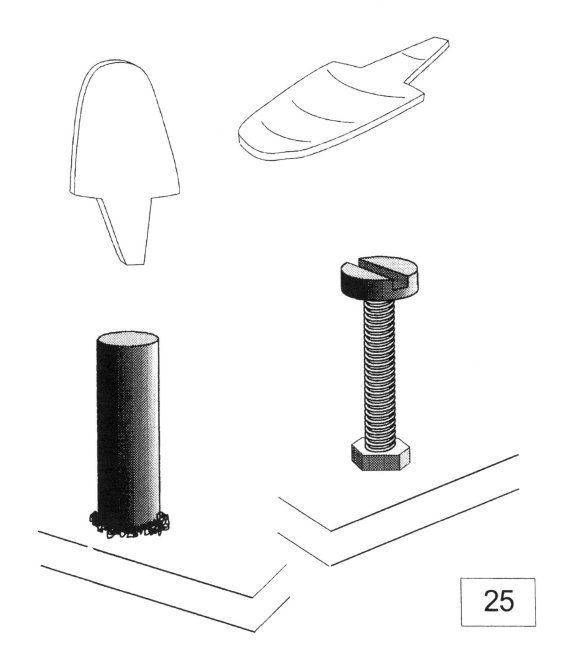

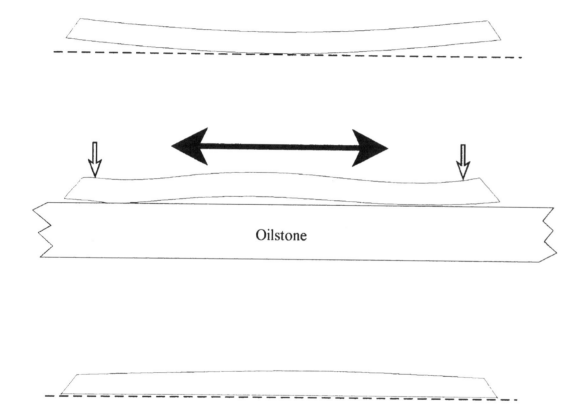

Oilstone

# The Details

### Mouthpiece

There are two main types of mouthpiece; those which have a flat underside and those which have a slot for the slider to run in.

I will deal with the first type to start with as it is easier to work on.

### #270 type mouthpiece

During manufacture the mouthpiece is intentionally bent to ensure even pressure along the length of the slide movement. If this has been done enthusiastically it can lead to air leaks (see diagram). The problem is that the curve overbends and you end up with air leaks in the centre of the instrument.

Use the rough side of the oilstone. Clamp firmly in a vice. Put the mouthpiece, underside down on the stone. Press very firmly down on the mouthpiece at the ends and slide it back and forward a few times on the stone.

Clean the ground face and have a look at it. You will see fresh grind marks a little way in from either end. The idea is to get a fairly uniform mark almost to the ends and just not in the middle. You must keep the same pressure all the time you are grinding otherwise the curve changes. Your thumbs will hurt a lot from this exercise.

When you have finished you should find that the ends are about 0.5 - 1.0 mm off the ground when you lay the mouthpiece on a flat surface. Anything around this is about right. When you screw the mouthpiece down there should be only a minimal air leak. Now you need to break all the underside edges slightly, especially the long side edges and corners.

Sometimes the underside hole edges obscure a portion of the slide holes resulting in reduced airflow. You need to file a small amount of material from the inside of each hole. The diagram shows you what should be removed. Watch that you take nothing from the mouth side of the hole, these are the right shape already (almost). With square hole mouthpieces there is a small benefit from breaking the corners of the mouth side of the holes. Do not do the obvious thing and make a nicely rounded edge here. The greater the rounding, the less 'feel' the tongue has on the hole and the less accurate the playing. This may be a personal thing and is well worth experimenting with.

When you have finished with this piece it will have to be plated.

I like to fill in any spaces in the mouthpiece with beeswax. The two areas are where the screws penetrate The lower end is easy .. fill and scrape flat. The spring end is not so easy as you have to cut out a channel in the wax for the spring to move in. The easy way is to put three or four slivers of card into the spring slot extending as far as the screw hole. When you have the wax in place and has set hard, take out the centre piece of card and the other two will fall out easily.

When you fit the mouthpiece back, do it this way. Slightly undo the retaining screws, ensure that the mouthpiece is central on the slide movement and that the slide movement is central on the body. Check that the whole assembly is positioned correctly end to end. Tighten the screws until they are 'finger tight'. This means that, when using a small screwdriver between thumb and forefinger, tighten until resistance is felt. At this point the mouthpiece should have settled flat with no air gaps. Now give the screw 1/8 turn extra, no more. If you find that you need to do more, then your engineering is wrong and you will have to check all the bits for flatness yet again.

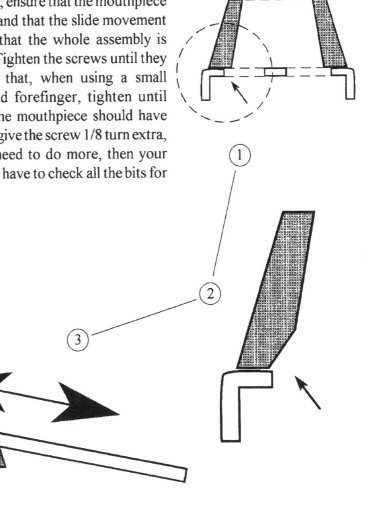

File

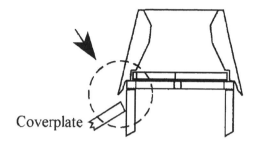

Coverplate

**Note.** The wax needs to be hot enough to flow into the cracks

Stiff wood, grain running from board to mouthpiece

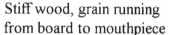

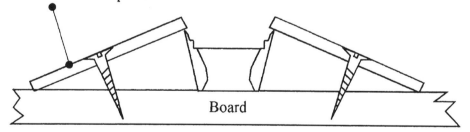

Board

## Amadeus type mouthpiece

This type of mouthpiece is used on the Meisterklasse and maybe others. In general they are a little better made than the previous type as they serve a dual purpose, mouthpiece and part of the slide mechanism. There is not a great deal to do to them but that bit is vital.

Although the manufacture is better, the concept of the design leaves a lot to be desired. The whole mouthpiece / slider unit is very insecurely held and tends to slip from side to side causing all sorts of air leak problems. Positioning and holding with a fillet of beeswax all along the cover to mouthpiece join helps a great deal but is not perfect. (see diagram and also Finishing Off at the end of the book)

Anything you do to this type of mouthpiece can very easily lead to disaster so please think carefully about what you are going to do before doing it!

Frequently I have found that the central slot in which the slider runs is too deep. Also, the floor of the slot is not flat. This mouthpiece does not take kindly to any alteration to its curve, so don't try playing with it. The mouthpiece must be clamped on your board so that the slight curve is taken out so that you can work on it. A way of doing this is shown opposite. You must use an accurately flat piece of metal (or stiff wood), glue 240 grit wet and dry paper to it and use this for filing the floor of the slot. You must do this with care. The metal must be only about 0.01" (0.025mm) smaller than the slot width and the paper must be cut to the edge. Do not under any circumstances try using W & D paper wrapped round a flat surface. The rounded edges of the paper will give a rounded edge to the slot. This in turn leads to the slide wedging as it approaches the side of the slot.

How do you know when the bottom of the slot is flat. Answer, you don't. What you can do is to get some 'Engineer's Blue' (a small tube). Smear a tiny amount on the flat piece of metal you are using for filing. Now rub this in the slot and you will see where the high points are. I do not use this method but watch what is being taken off as I file and judge when it is flat enough. Not so accurate, but possibly sufficient.

Even more difficult is to get the support ridges at the sides the correct height. They must be the same height and not slope inwards. A method I have found to work involves having a piece of hardened metal exactly the same size as the slider in width and about 0.007" (0.018mm) thicker than the slide you are using. Remember that this will be the size after any alterations you have made to the slider. You can use an old slider plus paper to pack it to size but this is less satisfactory. You need to use a file here, I have found that the W & D is not satisfactory.

Take care. Remember, you can always take off a little more later. It is slightly more difficult to file a bit back on! A word of warning.

You will need to get the mouthpiece Silver plated after this work. Make certain that the plating shop do not put silver plating on the underside. Ask them to flash chrome (or something else hard which will not add more than about 0.0002" (0.0006mm) material. Then on the rest of the mouthpiece you want a generous plating of silver. The problem is that if you get silver in the slide slot after you have worked on it, you won't be able to get the slider in the slot on a well made instrument! I speak from frustrating experience.

## Slide Movement

After the reeds the single most important part of the whole harmonica to get right is the slide movement. The quality of the movement and the air tightness of the mechanism are vital and fundamental to the production of good sound.

In each mouthpiece hole there is the capability of playing four notes, two blow and two draw. At any one time only one pair of these notes is available. The slide movement is the mechanism which directs air to the alternate pair. The general principle is that there are two 'white' notes available when the slide rests in its home position. When the slider is pressed two notes a semitone higher are allowed to sound. A simple way of putting this is that the slide gives you the sharp of the note you are playing.

If the player is to have real control of the sound then the mechanism must be very free acting and return fast when released. The obvious way to make it free is to give plenty of clearance on the moving part. The trouble is that the more clearance, the more air leaks away from the note you want and along the slide movement into other holes. This leads to a weaker sound and less control of the note.

### *Here is an interesting rough calculation.*

In the middle range of the harmonica the reeds are approximately 0.5 inches long (0.5"). The perimeter of the free reed is therefore approximately 1". The gap between the edge of the reed plate and the reed is about .002". This gives a lost amount of wind at about 0.002 square inches. This area is about doubled by the gap at the end of the reed.

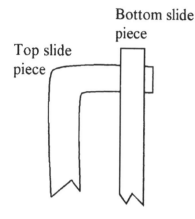

Top slide piece

Bottom slide piece

After filing

The slide movement is about 0.5" wide and the standard clearance is 0.012". So the gap down the slide is about 0.5 X 2 X 0.012 = 0.012 square inches. From this it can be seen that about 3 to 4 times the amount of air is lost down the slide as through the reed. Sure, there are other factors like saliva and reed movement, but it does explain why a good tight slide movement makes an instrument more responsive and gives it a better sound.

### Starters

Here is something you can do to make the slide much more comfortable in use but not to increase its functionality.

A small amount of Vaseline smeared top and bottom of the slider and worked into the slot by pressing the button a few times will make the movement feel smoother . Try also squeezing a small amount into the non-button end. Do remember to wipe off any surplus as it tastes pretty foul and does not improve ones concentration.

### Get out that file

There are several operations you can perform on the slide movement.

### #270, old style slider.

For over half a century the lower slide member has been made so that it overlaps and sticks out from the upper slider piece (U shaped bit). There are three locating lugs on each side if the unit and these fit into three slots on the lower piece. These slots are sharp and can cut your lips badly when playing.

The first thing to do is to clamp together the two outside pieces of the slide movement. Hold these firmly in a vice and file off the overhang on the bottom member. When you have this part flush with the top part there will be sharp edges. These have to be rounded. You can do this with fine wet and dry paper (about 400 grit) or carefully use a small file. Make certain that all sharp edges are removed as they can be very damaging to your mouth.

The next stage is to flatten the three pieces of the movement. When the pieces are punched out of a sheet of plated brass they dish. (shown exaggerated!)

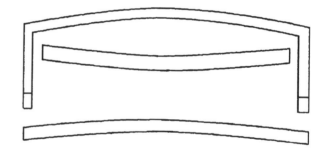

This means that they do not fit together snugly and there are quite large air leaks along the length of the slider. It is easy to flatten the slider and bottom piece, but the top piece is a little more tricky! If you do this alteration be prepared to have the pieces nickel or chrome plated afterwards, this is for health reasons as well as wear.

First take the button off the end of the slider. This is sometimes an easy job as it quite frequently falls off by itself! If removing the button proves difficult, clamp the slider in a vice and lever the button off with two flat-bladed screwdrivers. Now, for real ease of working you need to make a small wooden jig.

Get a piece of wood which has one side good and flat. You need about a dozen small nails, with only a small head or no head at all. Take an old lower slide movement piece and hammer nails into the wood round the outside of it. It should be nested and only have enough movement to allow it to be taken in and out. Hammer the nails down so that they are flush, or below flush with the surface of the slider piece. Now all you have to do is to hold the wood in the vice and you can work on the slide pieces.

With the lower slide piece clamped as described, use either a file or the oilstone to sweep over the surface of the material. You will find that you either take material from the centre of the piece or the two edges, it just depends on which way up you have it. Keep grinding until about half the surface area shows grind marks. Turn the piece over and do the same on the other side. Keep turning the piece over and taking a bit off each side until you can see brass over the majority of the surface area. The reason for not just doing one side completely first is that the material changes the bow as you grind off the plating. This method means that you take off a minimum amount of metal.

Now do the same for the slider. You may feel that you want to make a new nail jig for this piece as it is a slightly different size. However, you could get away with using the old one with a couple more nails down one side.

The top slide piece presents more of a challenge! There are three operations to do on this bit. Flatten the top. Easy. Flatten the inside. This is not so easy. You also need to reduce the height of the sides because the slider is now a little thinner and because you want a snug fit. Surprisingly this is not so difficult.

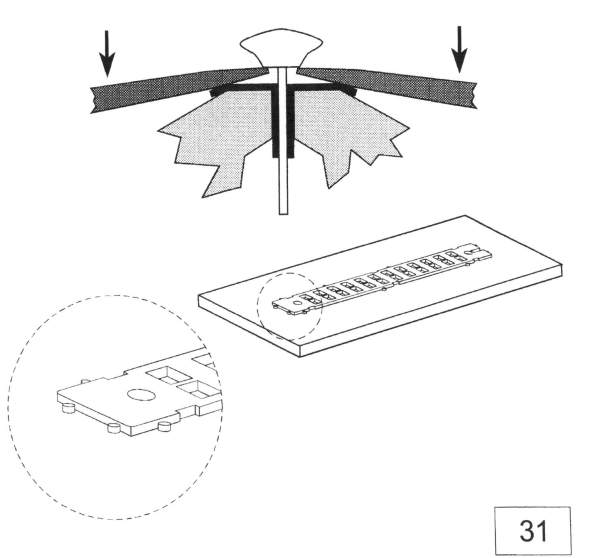

31

# Make Your *Harmonica Work Better*

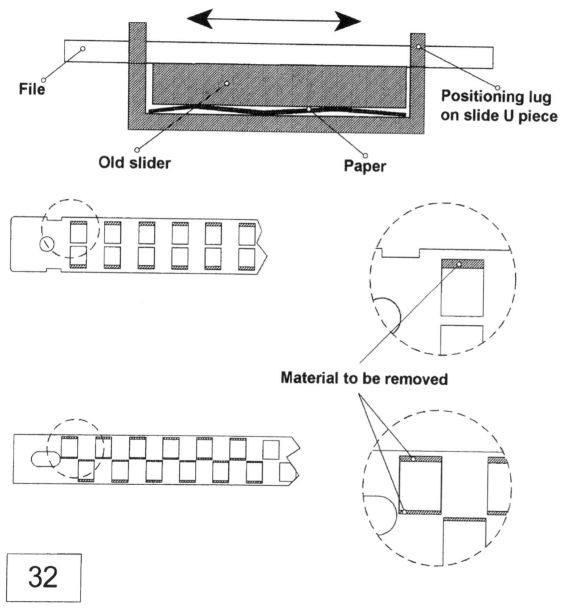

**File**

**Positioning lug on slide U piece**

**Old slider**

**Paper**

**Material to be removed**

You will need to do a new nail bed for the top flattening as the end nails will not hold the thing in place. Remember that you will alternate between flattening the top and the inside. To flatten the inside you will need either a flat file which exactly fits inside the slide slot or an oil stone which does the same. They are not too difficult to obtain. The inside has long shallow slot at either side of the inside which run the whole length of the movement. Try not to grind so much off that these disappear, if you do, the slide will not feel so free.

Now the difficult bit, lowering the sides by exactly the right amount.

For this you will need an old slider and a piece of newspaper. Cut a thin strip of newspaper to just fit in the whole length of the slot. Now put the old slider on top of this. The combined height of these two is just the height you need for the sides of the U piece. They will be used as a filing guide. Very carefully file down both sides of the U piece at the same time. You will find the job easier if you watch the old slider and see how you are touching this.

Eventually you will be filing both sides and just scraping the surface of the slider. Do keep the file parallel to the line of the U piece, don't rock it. When you have finished be sure to break the corners to take off the sharp edges. Take a little off each of the locating lugs otherwise they could rest on the reed plates and you don't want that!

Another job I like to do here is to break the edges of all the holes of the complete assembly, (60 holes, 4 edges, two sides = 480 edges!) Also attempt to do the same to the two slots on the slider, this will make the buffer tubes last longer. Take the sharp edges off the end and outside edges of the slider.

Before we leave this type of slide movement there is one other alteration you can make which can have a dramatic effect on the power and control of the sound. Increase the size of the holes up to about hole #6. This is a fiddly job more than difficult. Accuracy is good but not essential!

If you put a slider in the channel piece and wiggle it side to side you will notice that there is some overlap of the hole edges. In fact, on some slide movements I have come across, there is up to about 10% loss of air through the system because of this. This means loss of tone and power. The situation can be improved by extending the holes in all three pieces outwards. How much? If you look at the channel piece you will see small grooves down the edge of the channel. Extend the holes to these channels. The other two pieces can go a small amount more. Watch that you do not get out of parallel on the slider piece as this could seriously weaken the unit. The slider itself could have the holes enlarged towards the centre a small amount as well as towards the outside. This allows for the lateral movement of this unit.

Now you need to get the whole lot plated. Look for electroplating, or metal coating firms in your Yellow Pages. I favour 'flash chrome' because I have only ever had to get it done once!. Others have tried silver, gold etc. but it does not last. Recently there have been experiments in using PTFE (nonstick material in frying pans.) . Whatever you get done it is a good idea to wait until you have a few pieces to do . These firms usually have a quite high 'minimum charge' for private individuals and you can usually get 4 - 5 bits done for the same cost as one. If you do get one of the harder metals plated on the slider (flash chrome etc.) it is wise to make certain that the spring hole is well rounded on the top and underside. If you

do not do this the slider will eventually wear its way through the spring.

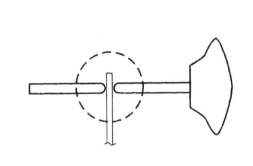 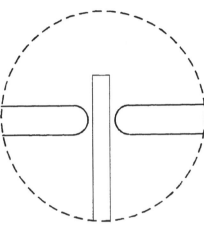

## Slide Buffers

I have only come across two types of buffer, the 'normal' tube and the rather ridiculous 'T' shaped Amadeus version. Let me explain the last statement. The action of the buffer is twofold; it helps to hold the mouthpiece and slide members in place by slotting into a hole in the body, and provides a semi-silent end buffer for the central slide. The normal sized buffer is of small diameter and is not very good at preventing movement laterally of the mouthpiece etc. The Amadeus buffer tries to overcome this by having a larger diameter portion which slots into a larger hole in the body. The larger diameter gives more support to the slide movement and makes the thing more stable. The problem is that the buffer is made of a rubbery material which gets cut to ribbons by the slide movement in a very short time. (A week in the case of both the instruments I have had)

33

# Make Your Harmonica Work Better

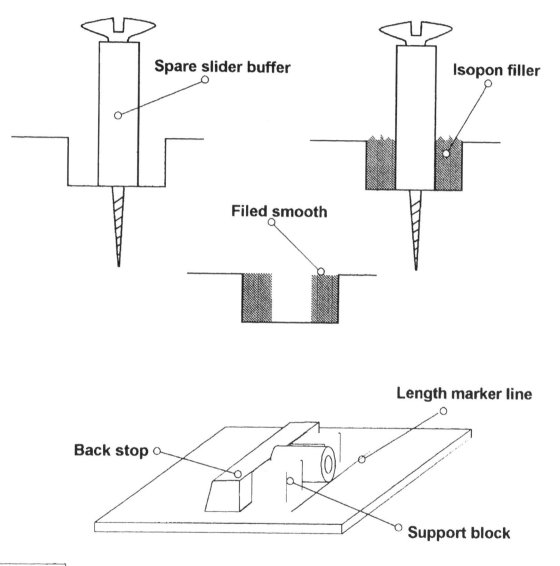

**Spare slider buffer**

**Isopon filler**

**Filed smooth**

**Length marker line**

**Back stop**

**Support block**

In the case of the Amadeus mouth organ do the following. Take a normal buffer, smear it lightly with Vaseline and screw it into position in the body (you can do both ends together). Mix up some Isopon (car body filler) and pack it in round the buffer. Scrape away any excess leaving the surface level with the front of the body. Leave for about 10 minutes to harden then unscrew the buffer and carefully take it out. This of course leaves a correctly sized hole which will take a standard buffer.

The standard buffers go hard and after a time they start clicking. The problem then is that the only way to improve the situation is to throw them away and replace. Some manufacturers do not even supply buffers which fit their own instruments so going back to them is frequently a waste of time. Solutions. Try model shops, they frequently stock soft neoprene tubing for fuel lines for model engines. Medical supply houses have either neoprene or nylon type tubing for dripping things into your bloodstream. However, the classic solution is to search all your friends ball point pens. The ink tube is usually the right size both internally and externally but some are made of harder material than others. Don't worry, there is always a couple of centimetres which has not got ink in so you will not have a blue mouth when you play.

The most difficult trick is getting the length of the buffer exactly right. I go to rather extreme lengths to make certain that there is a good fit as it helps with the stability of the whole movement. Make a little jig, just a small piece of wood with a another bar of wood on it to make an end stop. You can mark on this the exact length for a particular mouth organ (this has to be by trial and error). Butt the buffer up to the end stop and roll it under a Stanley knife blade at the exact mark.

NOTE, do not cut directly through, roll the buffer. This way the tube has a square end, direct cutting is difficult and normally gives a slanted end. I usually do a few at a time and slot the spares onto a toothpick or a piece of string so that they don't get lost.

If you have worked on the slider and body as described elsewhere the buffers should last 'forever'. Don't go changing them just because it is Sunday. Leave the mouth organ to mature!

## Slide knob

This item is ignored by most people but it is vital to the ease and comfort of playing. For example, some people find that the positioning of the knob on the Amadeus is too far out. It looks dramatic but does not work so well. However the position which is right for you will depend on your style of playing and the size of your hands.

A simple job is to re-glue the knob in position. Frequently the thing falls off. Clear all the old glue out of the hole and roughen the inside with a file or pin. Use an epoxy resin glue to fix it back onto the slide. If you are going to do anything at all to the slide movement wait until afterwards to do the job.

I find that the knob is too slippery for my playing style. It is a fairly easy job to serrate the end with a file or hacksaw and then smooth the whole thing off with wet and dry paper. If you have the equipment to do it a hollow in the end of the knob can be effective. Now to details of how to do the serrations. Make certain that all other jobs have been done on the slider and that the knob is firmly glued in place. Now place the slide in a folded piece of card and hold firmly in the vice with the knob resting on the top of the jaws. With a new

hacksaw blade in a small 'hobby' or 'junior' hacksaw make 4 cuts at 45°. These not be too deep, just enough to reach about ¾ of the way across the top of the knob. Now comes the tricky part. The straight slots have to be turned into V shaped grooves. You can do this with a square, rectangular or triangular file. Take care keep the angle of the file constant so that the walls of the groove are equal. This does not matter a jot so far as your harmonica technique is concerned, but it does look better if they are all even. Rock the file slightly front to back as you work to give a slight curve across the knob surface. When all this is done break the corners well. Your finger has to be comfortable, but I will bet it never slips again.

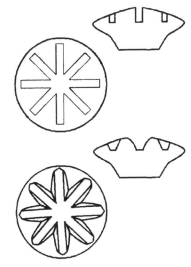

## Spring

The spring material is about right in most instruments. The way the spring is set up is wrong in nearly every instrument. The material itself is ordinary spring steel and so it goes rusty and eventually breaks. I have stopped using the standard springs and now use an ordinary commercially available safety pin! These are lightly plated and last for ages. They also seem to be about the right strength. You need to experiment.

The spring which arrives with your instrument can be very much improved (see diagrams on page 34). The coils of the spring are tightly wound together and rub against each other when the spring is operated making the action stiffer than necessary. The distance between the coils may be eased by forcing a thin domestic knife between the coils. You only need to be able to put a piece of newspaper between the coils. There is no need for a large gap. You may get away with twisting the knife once round all the coils.

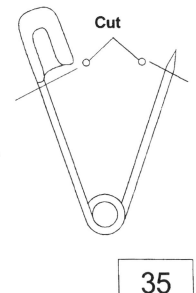

Cut

35

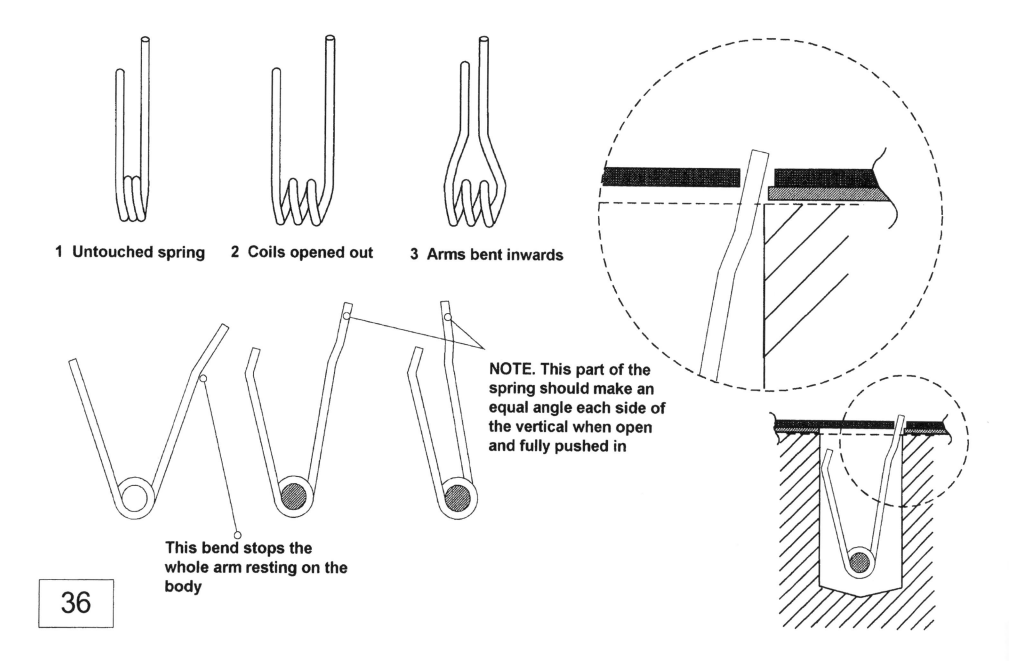

**1 Untouched spring** **2 Coils opened out** **3 Arms bent inwards**

NOTE. This part of the spring should make an equal angle each side of the vertical when open and fully pushed in

This bend stops the whole arm resting on the body

The spring also twists on the spring post as it is depressed because the two arms are offset from each other. You can reduce the twist by putting bends in the materials. This is best explained by the pictures.

You need to use the flat nosed pliers and vice for this job. Be careful how you go about putting the bends in the spring. Always put a little bend in first and gradually increase it until it is right. You will damage the structure of the material if you overdo the bends and have to re-bend back again. Go slowly and check frequently.

A small bend at the end of the short arm will help to stop this part of the wire digging into the body material and causing a little extra stiffness. This moves when the spring is used and is a point for lubrication.

The longer arm usually has a bend in it and this can be left alone. However the end of the spring leans a little too far backwards and does not go through the hole in the slider at right angles. The angle changes as the slide is pushed in so a little experiment is needed to find the angle and get it exactly right half way along the slide travel.

Now that the shape of the spring has been change you will have to find out what it feels like on the instrument. You must do this after you have finished with any alterations to the slide movement.

The strength of a spring is a very personal thing and again you will have to experiment. Do you want to grow muscles and have a very effective return, or do you wish to have an easy push and a sluggish return. Funnily enough you may find that the alterations you have already done have altered the action so that it really works well already. In which case, 'if it ain't broke, don't fix it'!

## Spring Post

There really is very little you can do with the spring post. You will come across two different types. The older mouth organs have a mild steel pin which is supported by the reed plates. The pin is a fairly tight fit and the position is quite stable. Quite a number of the more modern instruments have either a post moulded into the body material or a flat headed screw tapped into the body.

All of these methods are good and work well. However (as always!) watch out for the diameter of the post. It should be a comfortably loose fit in the spring coils but not very sloppy. A poor fit here allows for twisting of the whole spring which, in turn, slows down the action.

You are on your own here. There are several ways to approach the job. One is to make a spring post the right size and then fit it into the reed plates or body. This involves either a lathe to make it yourself or searching model shops for bits. In either case you will need to have either a comprehensive set of drills or a taper broach to increase the size of the hole in the reed plates. You might also like to think about plating this item. There is not much wear on the pin but it does go rusty if left in the natural state.

### Confucius might very well have said

*However ..*
*watch out for the diameter of the post. It **should***
*be a*
*comfortably loose fit in the spring coils*
*but not very sloppy.*
*A poor fit allows for twisting of the whole spring*
*which, in turn, slows down the action*

# *Make Your Harmonica Work Better*

**Body**

At the very simple stage there is nothing which you can do to alter the function of the body. Some people like to round off the corners of the back to make it more comfortable for holding. This, does not improve the sound. However, a comfortable instrument is easier to play than an uncomfortable one.

The next stage involves taking off the reed plates and the spring mechanism. When the wooden bodies are made they are accurate, flat and the right size. As soon as you breathe into the instrument the body starts to swell. When you put it down it shrinks again. The problem is that it does not go back into the same shape and eventually there are air leaks. There is also the problem that when you take the reed plates off the body it warps, and then it is almost impossible to get the thing back into shape again. So what can we do?

First DON'T take off the reed plates if you are at all faint hearted. You can still make one effective alteration. Here it is.

Take off the coverplates and remove the spring post and spring. Now take off the mouthpiece and slide movement. Put the coverplates back on making certain that they are behind the slots in the front of the reed plates. Make certain that the plates are tightened down well.

Lay some 200 grit wet and dry paper on a flat surface. Take an HB pencil and cover the front of the wooden comb in pencil marks. Now rub this face firmly over the wet and dry paper. Keep a firm grip on the body and do not allow it to rock. After a few strokes check the front surface. You will be able to see if anything is being taken off the wood or only the brass reed plates. What you need to achieve is an absolutely flat surface. This will then fit snugly with the slide movement which you have doctored.

You must take care that you do not file off too much. When the harmonicas are made the fronts are 'filed' on a continuous belt of sandpaper to get them flat. The result is usually very heavy-handed and a lot of material is removed. There is a little slot running along the front of the reed plates for the cover plates to rest in and the sanding frequently takes off so much material that it breaks into this slot. This leaves a knife-edge and means that you have to be very careful when making it really flat.

When you have finished the flattening process smear a little Vaseline along the front of the wood. I am not certain that it does retard the wood swelling in the future but it seems a good thing to do!. If you have taken the reed plates off to do the next stage, then some sort of grain filler (Vaseline, yacht paint, Ronseal etc.) is a good idea and really does help. Just remember to give a VERY light sanding over the surfaces a couple of days later when the paint has really dried and the body settled down to its new shape.

If you decide to go the whole hog and flatten the surfaces under the reed plates take care. If you are not careful you will snap off the very thin wooden partitions between the slots. Another thing to watch is rounding off the sharp corners at the front of the harmonica. These must be kept a sharp right angle. Do this operation before replacing the reed plates and grinding the front face.

## A body building exercise

Now for a fairly major operation. I have only done this to metal and plastic bodied instruments but I see no real objection to working it on a wooden one.

Every time you change the direction of your breath you have to change the whole reed chamber from positive pressure to negative pressure. If the chamber is smaller, there is less air to move and less air can mean faster. So, we make the chamber smaller. A very clever man, who has the misfortune to be a friend of mine, calls them 'Tate Ramps'. So be it! Here is how to make Tate ramps.

First, what to do with your body. If wood, leave as is. If metal and you have a curve sweeping up towards the back in the actual chamber, try to get someone to mill it out for you so that you have virtually a rectangular chamber. The plastic mouth organs I have come across are OK as they are. You need some car body filler. I use Isopon. You need an old hacksaw blade. Break it in half and wrap some plastic tape round the non broken end so that you can hold it. You also need a sharp 0.25" ( 6mm ) chisel, preferably one with tapered sides.

You are now going to fill the slots up with Isopon. Rough the insides of the slots with coarse W & D paper. This will help the Isopon stick. It is helpful to put a piece of masking tape all along the front of the instrument to stop the stuff bulging out when you put it in the slots. Mix enough for about six slots only at a time. Work on one slot at a time. Smear the mixture around the slot so that the walls and floor are covered and fill it as near to the top as you can. You will not be able to get it smooth at this stage, don't worry. Now do the other five. If the paste begins to go hard before you have finished do not start a new slot. Get rid of it and mix a new lot. Always clean your mixing stick and mixing plate between mixes. If you contaminate a new mix with a bit of the old which has not set hard yet, the new will set quickly!

Do the whole of the mouth organ in stages allowing each group of slots to harden (20 minutes) before going on.

You now have a knobbly mouth organ and have to start getting it back into shape.

First job is to cut a divider within each slot. If you look at the pictures you will see that there are two ramps in each slot. One faces forwards the other backwards. The cut you will do is between each ramp. There is absolutely no need to do this cut, but it makes the following operations easier. In all the slots make a sloping cut so that eventually the saw blade just touches the top of the back and the bottom of the front. You now need to use the blade to scrape the cut lower into the slot. The distance down you go depends on how deep the back of your final slot is going to be. At the low end of the instrument and up to about hole five (12 hole chromatic) this will be to the floor of the slot. The cut then gets less until the top hole will only be half depth. You may have to adjust this depth later depending on your playing habits.

Isopon cuts like very stiff cheese. You have to use pressure and a sharp tool, but it does not splinter or crack. The first cuts are the most difficult, the job gets easier near the end.

With the chisel

Cut the height of the plastic down by 0.1" (2mm). Extreme care needed not to ruin the slot dividers. This height is to allow for the combined thickness of rivet plus flap at the back right and rivet at front left of the slot.

Cut 0.1" (2mm) from the front of the slot.

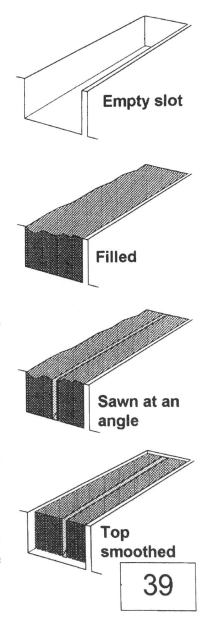

**Empty slot**

**Filled**

**Sawn at an angle**

**Top smoothed**

39

# Make Your Harmonica Work Better

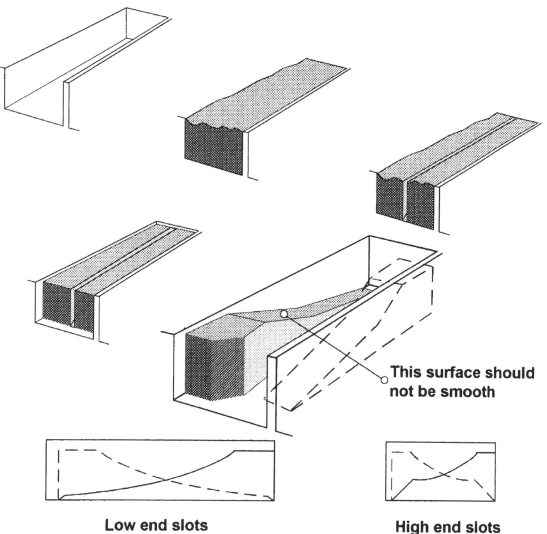

**This surface should not be smooth**

**Low end slots**

**High end slots**

Cut a vertical 45° angle cut at the front left of each slot to the full depth of the slot. This gives clearance for air coming in through the slider.

Starting about 0.25" (6mm) from the front and back start to create the two ramps. Looking from the front of the body the left hand ramp descends towards the back for the blow reed. Do check that the mouth organ you are working on has reeds in that order, otherwise you will be slightly frustrated in a few hours time. I advise roughing out the ramps on all slots at this stage. Then you can have a clean up of the work area before you begin on the fine work.

Things to watch.

On the lower holes, do get down to the full depth of the slot 3-4.. from the end.

Do not try to get a super smooth finish on the surface of the ramp. When the flap hits a ramp on a draw note you want as little surface contact as possible. Making the face like a mini roof top will eliminate any sticking.

You may find air holes in the Isopon. Just fill them in if they seem large, otherwise ignore them.

## Finished?

When you have finished, do not assemble and play. Wash carefully and then leave on a shelf somewhere for a week. The plastic needs to get rid of all its 'gas' which can be an irritant to some people. Please observe this, it really is for your own good. Putting it in a warm airing cupboard may help.

You should find that the instrument is far more responsive and firmer to play. Certainly, it works well for me.

## Reed Plates

There is nothing simple you can do to the reed plates with them still in position. Even if you take them off there is little to do unless you want a lot of hard work!

Something you can do which will aid the comfortable assembly of the whole instrument is to enlarge the two holes through which the cover holding screws pass. You need to enlarge it by about a millimetre. You can do this with a drill bit or with a file. If you do it with a drill bit the process is obvious. If you do it with a circular file then you don't need to widen the holes, only take about 1mm off the rear of the hole ( the bit closest to the back of the instrument.) Don't forget to break the edges of the holes afterwards. In fact it is a good idea to do it to every hole in sight.

The next stage, if you wish to go that far, is to take all the flaps off and doctor them (see under wind saving flaps)

You can make the reeds removable. There is a kit available from USA which enables you to make the reeds screw on and off.

Supplied by:-

Richard Farrell
PO Box 133
HARRISBURG
Ohio
43126 0133
USA

This is a wonderful idea and is well worth the money. If you decide to go this route then it is a good idea to flatten the reed plates.

When the plates are made there are some distortions due to the action of punching the slots in the plate. They are not very great, but they are big enough to make a difference IF YOU HAVE A NON-WOODEN BODY. If your harmonica has a wooden body it is not really worth the effort as the wood compensates by swelling.

To work on the plates you need to make a jig similar to the slider jig. A flat piece of wood a bit bigger than a plate which you can hold in the vice. Tap in nails all round a reed plate so that they are below the surface. Please remember that this is only done on a reed plate with no reeds on it!!! Now use the oil stone on its coarse side to take a bit off each side in turn until the majority of each surface shows flat (there will still be some small areas of the old tarnished surface showing). Do take care and do not take off too much. The thinner the plate becomes, the less stable it is and the thinner the sound becomes also.

To reassemble. Deal with the reeds as detailed in the American screw-reed kit. The flaps should be put on as detailed in the flaps section. One thing I would advise. Put on the flaps which are to be on the inside of the instrument and then assemble the plates on the body. Do any sanding of the front face of the mouth organ. Only when you have done this should you put the outside flaps on.

41

# Make Your *Harmonica* Work Better

## Reeds

First bit of advice. Leave well alone. The vast majority of instruments are manufactured to a very high standard. The reeds especially are extraordinarily accurate considering the small amount of time which is spent on them during assembly etc..

Second bit of advice. Now that you have decided to ignore the first bit of advice be warned, you are about to ruin some perfectly good and innocent reeds. Do not use your finest concert instrument for your first experiments. (I seem to spend my life saying this to people!)

## About reeds

This is the bit which makes the basic noise of the harmonica. The sound is thin, weak and uninteresting when the reed is 'pinged' with a finger nail on an open reed plate. However, put a body, coverplates, expert hands and expert air tract together with the plate and an enormous variety of tone colour and dynamic range are possible.

The reed itself is different to almost all other sound sources. It produces weird harmonics. When a string (violin, guitar) or a tube (trumpet, flute etc.) is forced to vibrate there is a fundamental speed at which the thing thrashes back and forward, be it air or string. Depending on where you hit the string or how hard you blow on a tube, a series of other notes are heard. These are called harmonics. Harmonics vibrate exactly at two, three, four, five, etc., times as fast as the fundamental note. Twice as fast produces a note one octave higher than the fundamental (C to an octave above C for example). Three times as fast gives, say C to G 1.5 octaves above. Four times gives two octaves and so on. As these 'harmonics' get higher they gradually go out of tune for a variety of reasons. For this reason trumpet players have to compensate their higher notes in a variety of ways. You can actually see all this happening on a guitar if you pluck the lowest string in various places.

I have tried to make this sound fairly simple, but the actuality is very complex. When you pluck a string it vibrates in a complicated manner which contains many of the harmonics at various 'volume' levels. It is this witches brew of harmonics which give an instrument its unique sound ( and why computers ain't quite got it right yet because it changes for every note!). For example a clarinet has a lot of 3rd, 7th, 8th, 9th, 10th harmonics whilst an oboe has a lot of 4th and 5th.

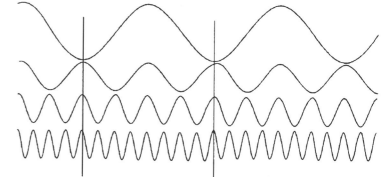

**Now to the free reed ..**

The 'harmonics' of a free reed are: The fundamental, f x 6.267, f x 17.55, f x 34.39. It says in 'The Electronic Music Manual' by Alan Douglas from which these figures are taken ".. *these overtones are clearly not harmonic; the first has a higher frequency than the sixth harmonic.*" You can say that again! This, I think, is why the sound of the harmonica is so rich, it is basically a noise generator which we can mould with hands etc. Pity the poor oboe or clarinet player with their woeful, standard set of harmonics!

Quoting again from the same source " .. *reed tongues must be carefully contoured,; any abrupt change in section causes a serious reduction in the safe range of stress. The surface finish .. has a decided effect on the fatigue range; the finer the surface, the greater the range ..*"

Various curves and tapers along the reed have been tried over the years, mainly in instruments like the Harmonium and Accordion. These have a far greater air pressure capability and the reeds tend to be made of steel rather than the brass type mixtures used for harmonicas.

Typically a harmonica reed is made as follows. A sheet of the reed material is held flat and then a channel is machined across it. The width of the channel depends on the final size of the reed and the length of the weight at the free end. This sheet then goes to a punch and many reeds of the same size are punched out of it. This whole process can be quite precise and the final reed will be either correctly in tune or only a little out. However, lets move in a little closer and look at this minor miracle. Close up you find that the back of the reed is smooth and the machined part is rough. If the reed has been tuned at the factory there will be a diagonal set of scratches across the reed. You may know that the easy way to cut a piece of glass in two is to use your diamond ring to draw a light scratch line across and then snap it. The glass breaks cleanly along the scratch line. It does this, not because the scratch is deep but because it is a discontinuity in an otherwise smooth surface. The same sort of thing happens with the scratches all along the reed. The result is not quite as dramatic as with glass but the end result is just as fatal! You have no doubt taken a piece of wire and bent it back and forwards to break it. Just before it breaks you can feel it weakening and see the point of the break change colour and become crystalline. This just what occurs with a reed. Unfortunately the scratching of the surface gives many points at which the stresses can be concentrated. The whole process is called metal fatigue. If you can get rid of this surface scratching, especially close to the root of the reed, the life will be extended considerably. You can do this but it takes a lot of time and effort, maybe about 15 minutes per reed. However, I did this to my #270 reeds in 1967. I will let you know when they start going drastically out of tune. (It is now 1994 and I think that 27 years is a reasonable lifetime for a busy reed!)

**Polishing reeds**

Materials needed.

A thin piece of stiff plastic sheet to put under the reed and support it.

A piece of 400 grit wet and dry paper (used dry even though on metal)

A piece of 800 or greater wet and dry paper

A flat needle file

Make certain that the reed plate is firmly held. A little jig

43

# Make Your Harmonica Work Better

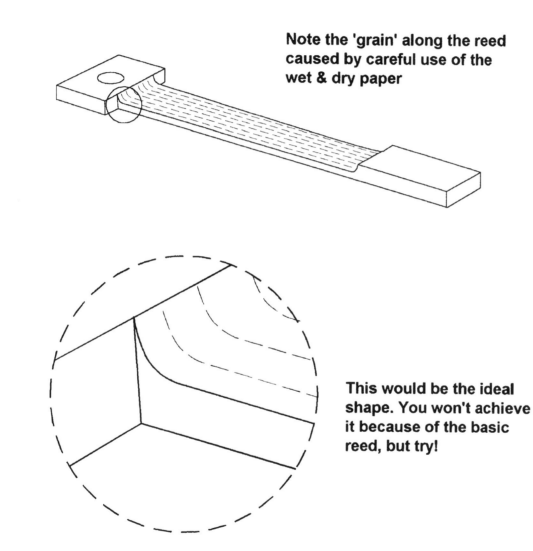

**Note the 'grain' along the reed caused by careful use of the wet & dry paper**

**This would be the ideal shape. You won't achieve it because of the basic reed, but try!**

as mentioned earlier is useful. You are going to need both hands and haven't got time to be bothered with holding the reed plate.

Ease the plastic sheet under the reed you are going to work on. Notice .. EASE .. do not force the reed to take up a new position. The plastic is to support the reed during working not to introduce new stresses. It is good if the sheet covers the surrounding reeds and flaps. (Really you should take the flaps off but confess that I did not when I first did it.)

With the needle file wrapped in 400 grit W&D, carefully smooth the top surface of the reed from root to tip. Only smooth in this direction. Try to get a rounded fillet at the root to reed join. Smooth until most of the scratching has gone then look carefully at the reed. If the remaining scratches look deep you must change the reed otherwise you will still have trouble. You must not take too much material off the reed otherwise it will never tune up again. When the reed is smooth on top, give it a rub with the 800 grit.

Now take out the plastic sheet and replace it with the 800 grit paper, grit towards the reed. The idea is to pull the paper out gently, twice. This will just break the corners on the underside of the reed. (You have already done them on the top because you were not good enough not too!)

Do this operation another 47 times.

Be very, very, *very*, *very* careful at the top end of the instrument. It is so easy to ruin these reeds and their settings.

## Tuning the reeds

The mouth organ is now very out of tune. So tune it! Only do not do it the way most repairers and the factories do it. You may find that the reed is very flat. This is easy to deal with. File a little off the weight end using the 400 grit wrapped round a flat file. Do not use the file, be subtle and take time. Better to approach being in tune than go to far and have to come back again. If you do go too far, don't take any more material off the reed body. The trick is to add a little weight back onto the end of the reed. A tiny spot of super glue is a good solution. (pun) You will have to wait about 20 minutes before you can test properly, and overnight before you can be certain of the final tuning.

How do you find out if the note is in tune? First, you do not have to be 'musical' to tune, but you do have to be able to hear well and concentrate hard! Tuning is a skill anyone can learn but some do better than others. If you find comparing notes between instruments difficult then there are electronic meters which will do the job for you with extreme accuracy. Such a meter will cost about half the price of a good chromatic instrument. You set the meter so that it emits a sound. Play the appropriate note on the mouth organ. If there is no difference in pitch the sound of the two notes will be clean. If the sound is grossly 'dirty' the tuning is a fair way out and you should be able to hear if the reed is lower or higher than the meter. As the notes get closer together you will begin to hear a beating effect and it is this beating that you use to get extreme accuracy. What you need to do is to tune the reed up or down until the beats disappear altogether, or maybe one beat every two seconds.

In my opinion the only way to find out if a note is in tune is to have the reed plate in an instrument, with cover plates on and to blow the thing in the same way you normally play it. As this is a lengthy process I look at all of the notes on the instrument with the thing together and write down a complete list of how each note is out of tune. i.e. G3 = 3 beats per second flat, Ab3 = very flat etc.

When the complete instrument has been logged, take it to bits. Hold the reed plate on a body and blow a note. Adjust the tuner so that it is the correct amount out of tune with the reed according to your list. Now tune the reed carefully as described above until it is in tune. This may seem weird, but the note sounded when the reed plate is held on and when it is properly placed is entirely different in pitch. This is a practical solution to a difficult problem.

If you really want to go to town on the tuning then you also ought to record what happens to the pitch when you blow softly and when you blow loudly. This will help you to tune for greatest accuracy. You will find that different reeds flatten to a greater or lesser extent over this range. I like to tune instruments about 2 beats sharp at A3 so that I can play into tune.

## Adjusting the set of a reed

The 'set' of a reed is to do with the way it sits in relation to the reed plate slot.

Any adjustment is a very delicate operation and must be treated with care.

Front to back adjustment is not really possible unless you remove the reed and either screw or glue it back in a different position. Sometimes the reeds do seem to be set a little too far back from the end of the slot. I believe that this contributes to

45

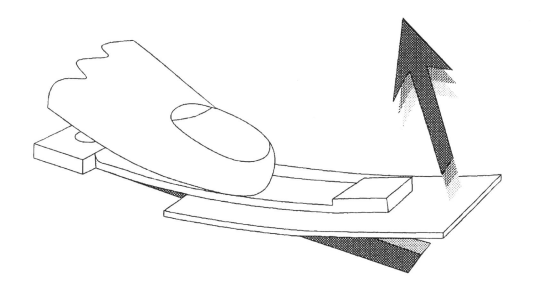

a breathy quality of a reed and lack of response. However, unless the positioning is grossly wrong and different from the other reeds, leave well alone.

Side to side adjustment. The reed is a fairly tight fit laterally. It may be swung slightly if the blade of the reed is not centrally placed in the slot. Hold the reed plate up to the light and you will get a very good idea of how well the reed is placed. Adjustment may be carried out by pushing on the side of the reed but I believe this is a dangerous pursuit. It is easy to distort the reed. I prefer to put a metal ruler against the back of the square root of the reed and twist it from here. It requires a bit of force as well as delicacy. This action also loosens the reed and after adjustment it would be wise to put a spot of super glue on a corner of this pad and the plate. The object is not to smother but discourage movement.

Height adjustment. This is a knotty one. The problem is that the reed may not be straight, it may have a curve in the length and this will alter the way you set it. The only real way of testing the set is to play the note. Does it clog up if you attack the note or just blow hard? If it does then the reed is possibly set too low. Does it just sound very breathy at low volume levels and will not work at all if approached lightly? This one is probably set too high, but check that it is not the flap sticking or the adjacent flap badly adjusted.

Adjusting a high reed is easier than a low. Just press near the base of the reed with the fleshy part of your thumb. The tip of the reed will dip into the slot as you do this and give you a guide as to how much pressure you are putting on. Now test and see how the reed reacts under all conditions. Do not alter so much that the reed is set too low! Only adjust enough to correct the condition of poor sound and slow starting. The idea of the fleshy part of the thumb is so that a pressure is put on a lot of the reed and not just a point. This way the reed will be less stressed and last longer.

Adjusting a low reed. There are two ways of doing this. The easy way can inflict stress damage on the reed. What you do is to put something like a credit card under the reed and push it towards the root of the reed. This pushes the tip of the reed upwards but is very difficult to control. I believe that it also puts stress on a very small area of the reed. The more difficult way is to use a thin piece of plastic or card about the thickness of a doubled up piece of exercise paper. Push it under the tip of the reed and gently ease it backwards towards the root until a little resistance is felt. At this point pull the card back about 1 mm. Put a finger on top of the reed and paper. Now gently raise the free end of the paper so that the tip of the reed raises against the finger. This has the effect of curving the reed along its length and creates a lot less stress. After you have ruined a couple of reeds you will find this a good way of doing the job.

An area for experiment is to see how the curve of the reed alters the sound. If a reed is curved so that the majority of its length is in the slot and only the tip stands proud, how does it sound? Some Harmonium reeds were twisted at the end to alter the sound. Some had the very end cocked up at about 30°.

Finally! Quite a few of the ills which seem to beset reeds as they get into middle age can be cured by a good wash (much like humans!). You can do this operation with the flaps on. I use rubber gloves, a dessertspoon of dishwasher powder and lukewarm water. Make certain that there are no granules undisolved in the water. Put the reed plate vertically in the water and swish it to and fro. The direction is at right angles to the plates surface. You can make some great waves! This forces the water through the slots. Do this for about 3-5 minutes. Yes, your arms get tired. Now wash in the same way with a few drops of washing up liquid. Do this for a couple of minutes. After this rinse in the same way with two changes of clear water. You will not foam at the mouth if you don't rinse well, but the instrument will taste foul.

## Rivets

Why is it that rivets appear to be made out of mild steel, which corrodes (rusts) in the damp interior of the harmonica? There really is no need for this type of sloppy design and manufacture. If your mouth organ has this type of rivet there are five things you can do.

> Put a spot of glue or paint over the exposed portion of the rivet
> Use the American bolt on kit mentioned elsewhere
> Change all the rivets for something in a corrosion resistant material
> Take out the rivets and glue the reeds on
> Throw the instrument away and get another type (!)

If you know how to rivet you will realise that this is a delicate job and very easy to mess up. Do not attempt if you have not been trained in the art, the alternatives are easier and just as effective.

I find that glue is better than paint. Use the stuff you already have to glue on the flaps, it works on the other side of the reed plate! Don't forget to roughen the rivet and plate first to give a bit of purchase for the glue.

The bolt on kit is very popular in the States and deserves

47

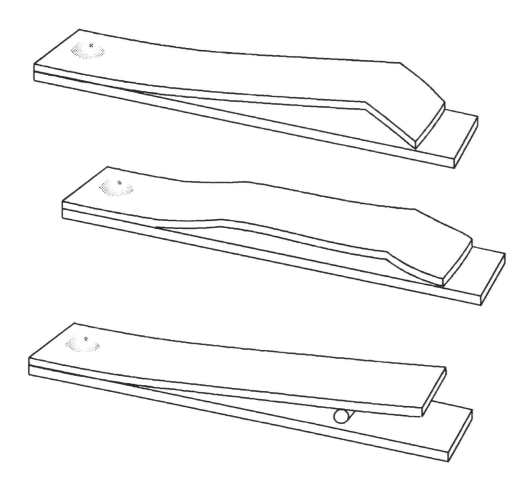

to be. Violinist and guitar players change their strings, oboe players spend half their lives making and changing reeds. Harmonica players in general try to find someone else to do their dirty work. If a job needs doing well have the arrogance to try it yourself, after all, you know exactly what you want. How to go about the job is fully explained in the kit.

Glue the reeds on? This is a rotten idea and difficult job and should only be tried in an emergency.

Throw the instrument away? I was joking. Never throw anything away. Try one of the alternatives.

## Wind Saving Valves (Flaps)

Good flaps are essential to a firm sound. If the flaps do not seat properly on the reed plate they will give a thin breathy sound.

All the flap does is to stop air going through the reed you are not using. The flap on the blow reed closes when you draw and the flap on the draw reed closes when you blow. Simple. However, making the things work well is quite difficult.

The flap must sit absolutely flat on the reed plate when it is closed and make an airtight joint. It must not move about when it is open but stay as still as possible so that it does not modulate the sound from the reed. When a reed is played softly the flap must lift cleanly and not stick. When the note stops the flap must seat down quickly and with no noise. The most common faults with flaps are buzzing when they should be closed and sticking when they should be opening.

Buzzing flaps are not seated properly. Usually you will find that the flap is slightly twisted along its length and one side is therefore slightly raised.

Sticking flaps are usually the result of a build up of saliva and / or other sticky substances. Another cause can be the top layer sticking to the bottom layer where the flap is the double type (most).

In both cases the easiest cure is to take off the flap and start with a fresh one. If you have no spares from old mouth organs then you will just have to refurbish. On rare occasions you may be able to persuade a manufacturer to sell you a set of various sizes which you can then cut to shape.

Luckily the majority of faulty flaps sit on the outside of the reed plate and are easier to get at. I think that this is probably due to the faster drying out of the external flaps. However, I have no concrete proof that this is the case.

### Removing a flap

A pair of flat nosed pliers are ideal for this purpose. I have glued a very thin layer of card to each jaw so that the surface is relatively soft. (you can also chamfer the edge of the card so that no sharp edges come into contact with the flap) If you grasp the flap for about half its length and pull parallel to the surface of the reed plate it will come away cleanly and remain straight and flat. If you pull it upwards the glued end will curl and present problems when you come to refit. You can also remove a flap with a razor blade under the glued end. I can never make this work but some players can.

### Preparing the reed plate for refitting a flap

When you have removed a flap there is always a lump of glue and a bit of torn flap left on the plate. Remove this with a razor blade or some other sharp tool.

I find the flaps on commercial instruments sometimes fall off. To prevent this happening I always roughen up the area round the rivet where the flap is glued with a small file. You can equally well do it with a pin or some such. This just gives a bit more purchase for the glue.

### Preparing a flap for refitting

Most flaps consist of two pieces. There is a fairly floppy piece with a slightly rough underside and a shiny top side. The other piece is much stiffer and made of a harder and shinier piece of plastic material. The floppy bit does the air sealing and its weakness allows it to fit itself to the plates irregularities. The top piece gives strength and speed of return. It also prevents the lower piece flying too high when lifted. Some instruments have leather flaps and I have heard of players who like them. Some people like driving Skodas.

Most flaps get sticky over the years and it is very difficult to stop it happening. I have heard of one 'cure' you might like to try, Victor Brooks suggested this one to me. What you do is to use a wax crayon on the underside of the flap. I have not tried it but he reports good results.

The way to remove any deposits which have caused sticking is simply soap and water. Lukewarm is good as your hands will like it. Hot is bad because the flap will curl up and die. Just lay the flap on a smooth surface and gently wipe the underside surface with a cloth from root to tip. After about a dozen strokes you can bet that most of the muck will be off. Sometimes the gap between the two pieces has become contaminated. Dealing with this is a little more difficult. I use a bit of newspaper, the lower the morals of the paper the more absorbent the actual paper seems to be. Carefully separate the two layers, put the paper between, squeeze lightly and pull the paper out. Do this a few times to clean it. After you have

49

# Make Your *Harmonica* Work *Better*

finished, rinse in cold water. Now you have to dry them. Lay them on newspaper face down and put a bit of newspaper between the two bits. Leave for a few minutes to dry off. It is a good idea to try and carefully clean around the reed slots where the flaps seat as there will be deposits there as well. In this case do not use anything abrasive as any roughness will hold the moisture and speed sticking.

I am sure that you will have realised that you don't have to take flaps off the reed plate. You can use the same method as cleaning between the layers for both jobs if the flap is still attached. However the more lengthy task is easier in the long run.

Getting rid of buzzing can be a real pain. It is difficult to untwist a valve which has taken on corkscrew characteristics. However, buzzing is not always caused by twisting. Sometimes it can be caused by the two layers sticking together just a little way off the surface of the plate. You know how to deal with that (see above). Another cause is the flap arching slightly away from the reed plate so that both ends are on the surface but the middle isn't. Usually an examination of the flap will show whether it is one of the causes already mentioned.

I would almost say, 'Clean and Try' will get you out of most flap troubles where they once worked!

An aside. I used to help Larry Adler with his instruments sometimes and they would come to me with the flaps looking as though they had been in heated curlers. He would push anything he happened to have handy inside the instrument to unstick a flap. They do not like it! Having said this he still made a heavenly sound with them. I think you could give Larry Adler a lump of concrete disguised as a mouth organ and he would still make a better sound than anyone else.

## Fitting the flap

Do I really need to say 'put a spot of glue on it and stick it down'? Yes I do. Use only a tiny spot of glue. Hold the free end of the flap and lay the glue spot exactly on the rivet. Press lightly with a spare finger and let go. Now quickly adjust the position of the flap so that the tip just conceals the end of the slot. Check that the flap sits equally on both sides of the slot. When dry, check that the glued end will not get in the way of the coverplate when it is fitted. If it will, make a vertical cut with the razor blade and remove the excess material and any glue in the same area.

## Things you can do to a flap to make it work better

Sometimes you can make a flap work faster and better by providing a small air gap between the two pieces of material. A couple of different methods are shown in the drawings. You can bend the top piece so that it only touches near the end. There are some dangers with this method but it is easy to do. You make the bend with the flat-nosed pliers. When I have used this method I usually put a piece of 400 grit wet and dry paper between the two pieces and take the sharp edges of the end of the upper piece. This will allow the top piece to slide smoothly over the bottom piece.

The second method involves sticking a small piece of cotton to the top piece. To do this put a tiny spot of glue on the top piece and lay the cotton across the glue when it is tacky. When the glue is completely dry cut off the surplus cotton on either side. Make certain that the glue does not get onto the bottom piece. Do not allow the glue to be thicker than the cotton.

Where the flaps end, usually at hole 10, is a matter of taste. Some people only have them up to hole 6 or 7 as they like the extra ability to bend notes. If you like to play fairly 'straight' music then the more holes flapped the better. I put flaps on all the reeds. This, in combination with the alterations you do to the slide movement, gives a wonderful pure sound to the upper register. When you go back to playing an instrument without these alterations, you realise that you have been playing something which sounds like a leaky tyre for years! A word of warning. Be very careful in this region of the instrument. The setting of the reeds in 11 and 12 is very touchy and very difficult to put right. Also the reeds are sometimes a little hard, especially in hole 12. If you have a reed in 11 or 12 which is excessively hard to operate, get a harmonica repairer to change the reed for you if you do not want to do it yourself, it is very worthwhile spending the money. Happy is the person who knows when to stop DIY and call in the expert! (Happier still is the person who is willing to experiment and mess up a few things in order to become an expert!)

## Cover Plates

There cannot be anything you can do to a coverplate, surely? Wrong, there are a surprising number of things which can be done to 'improve' the plates.

Some of the modern instruments have plates which appear to be made of stainless steel. These are excellent and work well. However, all plates can be improved by silver plating. There are two major benefits from this operation. First. Your fingers now do not slip on the plates but your lips do (the exact opposite is true of the traditional nickel-plated plates!).

Second. They look and feel great.

Before you rush out and get your plating done, look at the section on slides and mouthpiece. Getting the whole job done at once is much cheaper than getting things plated piecemeal.

Silver plating makes a remarkable difference to your playing comfort and attitude to the instrument. If you are to get the maximum benefit from your money there are some things you can do to make them even better.

Most cover plates suffer from having one or two sharp edges which need to be broken. They also do not seem to have a flat front end for sitting down on the reed plate. The Hohner #270 is a particular offender and I will describe what to do to that plate and you can watch out for similar types of poor manufacture on other harmonicas.

If you look at the front edge of the top plate at the end where the 12 is you will find that there is a slight bump which lifts the front by a few thousandths of an inch. This may not seem much but it allows a significant air leak at the front of the instrument. This needs to be ground off. There is sometimes a slight bump at the other end as well. To help get the whole thing really airtight it is a good idea to bow the plate a little so that the centre pushes down on the reed plate and keeps it firmly on the wood. These two jobs should be done at the same time with the curving being done before bump removal.

You can put a subtle curve into the plate with a little practice and a nasty kink with no practice at all. Hold the plate in both hands with the writing and the front edge towards you. Stroke the whole length of the plate along the portion which has the numbers on it. Do this with your right thumb while

51

supporting the plate in your left hand (if you are right handed). If you put a little pressure into your stroking you will achieve a nice gentle curve a couple of millimetres deep, no more. Now you need to use the oilstone to grind the underside of the plate to make it sit flat. Fix the stone into the vice, lubricate. Put the plate flat on the stone. Pressing fairly hard down on both ends of the plate with your thumbs, stroke the plate along the stone. This will reduce the curve a little and get rid of the bumps. You end up with a very flat front to the plate and a slight curve which flattens when screwed down. Break the edges.

The assembly of the complete mouth organ can sometimes be made better if the holes used by the holding down screws are elongated by about 1 - 2 mm towards the front of the plate. This allows the plate to be shifted backwards slightly.

At the rear of the plate there is a ridge made by the metal curling sharply round. This adds strength and stiffness to the plate and also gives a convenient place for the fingers to rest. Inside the plate, the ridge looks like a small wall getting in the way of the sound emerging from the back. I do not know whether or not this has a significant effect on the noise the instrument makes, but I always assume that it does and do something about it.

It is easy to file the inside of this ridge down so that it is level with the general line of the plate. This must not be overdone as it will reduce the strength of the plate. This still leaves a small trench in the plate and I usually fill this with beeswax or Isopon. I prefer the beeswax as it is easier to do, less messy and easy to remove if you don't like it!!

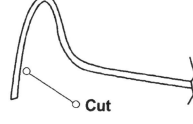

**Cut**

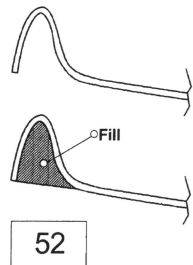

**Fill**

## Cover Posts

These little beasts are very underestimated in their usefulness. They have to be just the right height so that the coverplates are stressed for the right sound. They have to have a rounded and not too sharp end so that they do not dig into the coverplate. They need to be strong enough not to shift and bend and not so large that they obtrude into the sound passage out of the instrument. They need to enhance the look of the instrument.

Most cover posts are none of these things. On many instruments they are made out of pressed out brass. These bend and break at the slightest provocation and certainly do not provide any real support.

One solution is to glue a new spring post made of plastic rod to the reed plate using an epoxy resin. This is difficult to get right. Firstly, the post has to have a very flat and square bottom so that it stands upright. Secondly it is difficult to get the exact right height. I prefer to put a screw through the reed plate and into the body material. This can allow height adjustment and so lessen any stress on the reed plate. Further to this I put a rubber cap over the screw to give a springy support to the cover plates. You can make this cover out of a pencil eraser with a little ingenuity, a razor blade and a little artistry.

There is a product available which does the job very well. Hohner produce a glockenspiel called a Granton. This has rubber supports for the metal bars. These do very well and as the Granton is used in schools the kids are always eating them so there is a replacement service. A dozen of these should cost very little. They need cutting to length, but it is easy.

## Finishing off

You should now have a lot of harmonica pieces in good condition, or an instrument which you have just bought and want to make play well. This is possibly the most effective 'secret' of all and is the easiest.

With the instrument assembled and working better than you ever thought possible, get out the soldering iron and beeswax.

Lay the harmonica on a piece of crumpled cloth so that you can adjust it's position. The cover plate and mouthpiece need to be nearly horizontal, maybe a little downhill towards the mouthpiece. With the soldering iron making a hole in the beeswax, dribble some of it all the way along the join between cover and mouthpiece. Now do the same on the other side. Go back to the first side and slowly run the soldering iron along the bead of beeswax. The speed is slow, about an inch (2.5Cm) in 10 seconds. This helps to heat up the metal surround and allows the stuff to flow into crevices. When you have finished both sides, leave for about 20 minutes on a cool place. Now clear the excess wax off with a wooden spatula or thumb nail. Finish off by polishing the fillet. (see Using Beeswax at the start of this book)

## Finally

I hope that you have found this interesting. The harmonica is a wonderful instrument but it can be *so frustrating!*

Some frustrations are caused by our sheer inability to play the thing. However life is so much easier if the instrument itself is not adding to the burden of pain and woe.

If you have grasped the nettle and had a go at some of the techniques suggested above then it is down to you to play better! Don't let the harmonica down. Learn to play well.

Talking of playing well, just by coincidence, there is a book on this very subject ...... but more of that later!

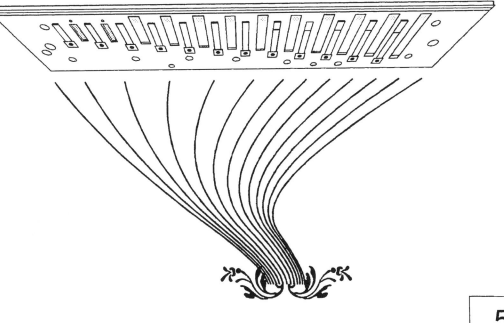

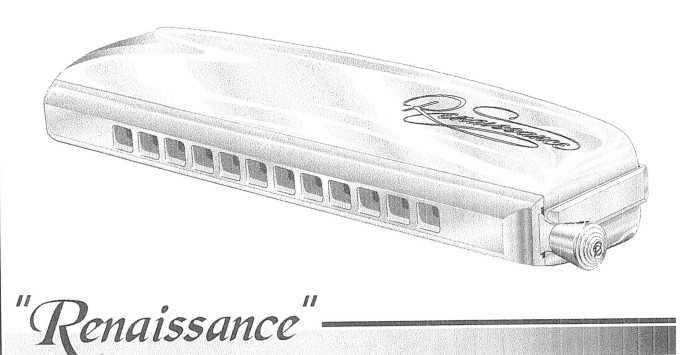

# You'll Like What You Hear!